Embassies of Washington

12/99

While many of these are attractive & each unique, Waterford enjoys the same attributes but has the advantage of a superb setting. Enjoy!

Greetings & warm wishes from
Cameron & May LaClair

EMBASSIES
of
WASHINGTON

CAROL M. HIGHSMITH AND TED LANDPHAIR

PHOTOGRAPHS BY
CAROL M. HIGHSMITH AND
DAVID PATTERSON

THE PRESERVATION PRESS

NATIONAL TRUST FOR
HISTORIC PRESERVATION

The Preservation Press
National Trust for Historic Preservation
1785 Massachusetts Avenue, Northwest
Washington, D.C. 20036

The National Trust for Historic Preservation is the only private, nonprofit organization chartered by Congress to encourage public participation in the preservation of sites, buildings, and objects significant in American history and culture. Support is provided by membership dues, endowment funds, contributions, and grants from federal agencies, including the U.S. Department of the Interior, under provisions of the National Historic Preservation Act of 1966. The opinions expressed here do not necessarily reflect the views or policies of the Interior Department. For information about membership in the National Trust, write to the Membership Office at the above address.

Printed in Singapore
96   95   94   93   92   5   4   3   2   1

Library of Congress Cataloging in Publication Data

Highsmith, Carol, 1946–
    Embassies of Washington / Carol M. Highsmith and Ted Landphair:
photographs by Carol M. Highsmith and David Patterson.
        p.   cm.
    Includes bibliographical references (p.   )
    1. Embassy buildings—Washington (D.C.)—History.
2. Washington (D.C.)—Buildings, structures, etc. I. Landphair,
Ted, 1942– . Patterson, David, 1960– . III. Title.
NA4443.W3H54 1992
725'.17—dc20 91-43141
ISBN 0-89133-170-0
ISBN 0-89133-190-5 (pbk.)

Contents

Acknowledgments

IT HAS BEEN A TREAT TO PRESENT, IN RICH PHOTO-graphic detail, the elegance and grandeur of the buildings that house the world's representatives in Washington. The diplomat's art has been employed with grace, not only by genial ambassadors and their hospitable spouses but also by the authors' associate, Dorothy M. Jones, whose charm opened many an embassy door and pried loose uncounted juicy details. The exquisite, and in some cases priceless, furnishings inside these buildings overwhelm the visitor, but extraordinary skill was required to arrange and light them in ways that evoke their splendor for readers of this book. Our photographic associates, Dave Hofeling and Neil Greentree, were masters at doing so.

Turning up the delicious stories of many of these properties proved equally challenging. You might think that an embassy staff would know all about the eccentric or ostentatious history of its building, but more often the here-today, gone-tomorrow diplomatic inhabitants haven't a clue. Wonderful studies by writer Hope Ridings Miller, the U.S. Commission of Fine Arts, and others have focused on some, but not many, of the embassies in detail.

When, for instance, the authors discovered that not one but two of the grand ambassadorial residences—of France and Portugal—had been built for the same man, a hitherto obscure figure named W. W. Lawrence, we were determined to learn more about him. That particular search took us to the Colorado mining territory, to Pittsburgh, where Lawrence and his father started a paint company, and to New York, where he and his wife hobnobbed in high society. It took some real spadework to uncover the reason this man of Pennsylvania and New York would build two luxurious Kalorama homes. For help in tracking down just that one elusive businessman, we are indebted to Princeton University archivist Ben Primer; to Harold Moldan, manager of the Sherwin-Williams Corporation's records division in Cleveland; to Walter Kidney, historian at the Pittsburgh History and Landmarks Foundation; and to Carl Miller at the mining museum in Leadville, Colorado.

Bruce Moffat at the Chicago Transit Commission gave us an enormous breakthrough in pinpointing another shadowy figure, Louis Owsley, who built the home that became the embassy of the Netherlands. John Hodges, archivist at the Navy Historical Center at the Washington Navy Yard, put us on the scent of Captain Thomas Moran, first owner of the residence now housing the Ecuadorian ambassador.

The wealth of broader research began with a thorough thumb-through of the marvelous programs of the Davis Memorial Goodwill Industries' embassy tours and galas, featuring Allison Brown's elegant sketches, which were cheerfully made available by Goodwill public relations manager Ruth P. Howard and explained by supervolunteer Mary Cavett Sims.

Deeper, rolled-up-sleeves-variety research was made pleasurable by a host of accommodating experts, including architect Francis Donald Lethbridge, who had been part of a survey of great Washington buildings; Joseph Mancias, Lee Feldman, Donald Jackson, and especially "institutional memory" George Oberlander of the National Capital Planning Commission, the agency in charge of managing the spread of chanceries; and Sue Kohler, historian for the U.S. Commission of Fine Arts, who helped produce four fact-filled volumes on Massachusetts Avenue and 16th Street houses.

Others who graciously opened treasure troves of information from their files included Orden Lantz, curator at the National Park Service's National Register of Historic Places; D.C. Public Library Washingtoniana Division librarians Matthew Gilmore, Mary Ternes, and Roxanna Dean; David Maloney of the D.C. Office of Historical Preservation; William Kay, a volunteer staff member, and curator Cheryl Miller, his supervisor, at the Historical Society of Washington library; George Caldwell at the Library of Congress; Carol Twombley, chief of the American Institute of Architects' library; Frank Aucella and Michael Sheehan at the National Trust for Historic Preservation's Wilson House; Howard Berger and Ann Hargrove of the Sheridan-Kalorama Citizens' Association; and Wayne Quin of the law firm Wilkes, Artis, Hedrick & Lane. Thanks, too, to Dick Pearson, Smith Wood, and Jackie Fleisher-Wood for being there when we needed them.

Finally, a special word of thanks to Hope Miller, the quintessential chronicler of the embassy scene, for her personal insights, guidance, and encouragement of our project. We trust that the final product slakes the curiosity of those who simply want to peer into the embassy world as well as those who crave richer information. Putting the package together has been a wonderful, collaborative experience.

Ted Landphair and Carol M. Highsmith

The photography was made possible by WASHINGTON FLYER magazine. Greenworks by Shane Floral, Inc., provided floral arrangements used in interior views of embassies.

Introduction

IT WAS AMERICANS, QUITE POSSIBLY PUTTING ON airs, who developed the notion that the great homes of foreign ambassadors should be called "embassies." Abroad, an embassy had traditionally been what Yankees call a "chancery," a utilitarian office for the paperwork business of state. But to an American visiting Washington to see the sights, an embassy has always meant that imposing, implicitly off-limits mansion where elegant dinners are spread; theme soirees thrown; dinner jackets, lavish gowns, and precious gems paraded; fine wines and finer cigars tasted; exotic tongues spoken; and fabulous furnishings from distant places savored. Even in times of international austerity this is not a fanciful picture. Just such an opulent world still swirls behind the wrought-iron gates and heavy oak doors of diplomatic Washington today. In *Embassies of Washington,* we pass through those gateways and open those doors to linger at some of these great homes — and several of the memorable chanceries as well.

Originally the word "embassy" had nothing to do with stone and mortar. An "ambassy" or "embassie" meant the envoy's affairs, or the retinue that carried them out. In *Love's Labour's Lost,* Shakespeare wrote, "Here comes in Embassie The French King's daughter." Sir William Temple in 1669 talked of "Lord Falconbridge, who is going on Embassy."

"Going on Embassy" was an idea grandly seized later that century by Peter the Great of Russia, who, after his ship almost foundered in the Baltic Sea, vowed to travel to the tomb of his patron saint in Rome to thank God for his deliverance. Ignoring the howls of his suspicious subjects and the insular Orthodox church, Peter had already opened Muscovy to foreign influence by cavorting in a "German quarter" of Moscow and employing Swiss officers like Francis Lefort to repel Tartar invaders. But when Peter launched the "Great Embassy," a journey through the western world to study customs, science, and shipbuilding, he set a never-equaled precedent for diplomatic junketing. Peter himself traveled incognito, as much as was possible for a man almost seven feet tall surrounded by a phalanx of boyars and bodyguards. He and his minions spent eighteen months abroad, but he never saw Rome.

It was to such free-floating delegations that the 17th-century English poet John Milton referred when he wrote of "Embassies from regions far remote," or that historian William Hickling Prescott, as late as 1843, had in mind when he spoke of "the embassy, consisting of two Aztec nobles, accompanied by the governor" in his treatise, *The Conquest of Mexico.* Not until the mid-19th century did an embassy come to mean a center for diplomatic intercourse. "It was a brilliant ball at the Palazzo of the Austrian embassy at Naples," reported the English novelist Edward Bulwer-Lytton in 1837.

The ancient Greek city-states had sent missions to one another and even developed the first rules of protocol—the "formula of international politeness." Key to protocol was a prohibition on accepting tribute (Virgil, three centuries later, picked up the theme: "I fear Greeks, even when they bring gifts"). Greek emissaries were distinguished elders in the Plato mold, not a professional cadre.

Roman law established the concept of diplomatic immunity,

*Preceding pages:
Villa Firenze, the Tudor
residence of the Italian
ambassador, sits on 22
lush uptown acres that
had been the sixth most
valuable piece of private
property in Washington.*

which was finally codified centuries later in 1961 as part of a Vienna treaty. The Romans accepted far more ambassadors than they deigned to send. Until the French perfected the art of diplomacy, Latin, spoken as well as written, was the accepted language. Today both English and French are de rigueur for the cultivated foreign representative—French since the early 19th century.

In the Middle Ages, warring knights were more worried about repelling barbarian assaults than defining the rules of court, and papal representatives handled most of the world's diplomatic chores. But by the late 15th century, Italian principalities had set up a network parallel to that of the Church, dedicated, in the fashion of Florentine Niccolò Machiavelli's later model, to international intelligence and intrigue.

With the emergence of Europe's great monarchies came the ceremonial pomp and rigid code of etiquette that defined the diplomat's calling. France's King Francis I dispatched the world's first permanent foreign representatives in the early 1500s, and the French were also the first to employ career diplomats and to institute competitive foreign-service exams. But all was not always civil in this civil service. In 1661, as the British prepared to greet a new emissary from Sweden, a battle royal (fought with swords, not conversation) ensued between the Spanish and the French as to whose coach should lead the welcoming procession. Spain prevailed, and the outraged Louis XIV retaliated by throwing the Spanish ambassador out of Paris.

England had quickly followed France in establishing a department of foreign affairs, going the French one better by dividing its secretariat into northern and southern departments, the better to serve the far-flung empire. Not surprisingly, the Prussians under Premier Otto von Bismarck introduced the idea of using foreign posts to drum up mercantile opportunities.·

International diplomacy, with its ostentatious trappings, soon attracted pretenders among the lesser states, whose own representatives scurried around the globe, prompting the English writer Aldous Huxley to remark, "Official dignity tends to increase in inverse ration to the importance of the country in which the office is held." Rules of diplomatic precedence were first codified at the congresses of Vienna in 1815 and Aix-la-Chapelle three years later. The rules still apply. In Catholic countries, papal nuncios generally represent the various diplomatic delegations when a collective voice is needed; in other countries, the dean

At the Danish chancery, a self-portrait of the great uncle of the ambassador's wife sits on a lemonwood-inlaid oak secretary, carved in the 1700s in Schleswig-Holstein province.

of the corps is the ambassador of longest standing. In Washington, that senior ambassador also gets the coveted DPL-1 license tag for his or her automobile. The 19th-century congresses also defined the pecking order for emissaries: ambassador (full title: ambassador extraordinary and plenipotentiary), legate or nuncio, followed by the envoy or minister, with chargés d'affaires left to long for career advancement.

Until the 18th century, a minister generally did not travel abroad with his wife; thereafter, diplomatic privileges began to be extended to her as well as to the ambassador's top-level entourage. Only envoys who were persona grata were to be accepted by the nations to which they were assigned, though over the years all sorts of scoundrels have been welcomed with a flourish. Rejection or expulsion was rare until the Cold War, when ambassadors and their staffs, some of whom were exposed as dandified spies, were sent packing in tit-for-tat flurries.

The United States did not get around to sending full ambassadors abroad, or accepting them, until 1893—more than a century after the nation's founding. Ministers, operating from legations, had previously been the highest-ranking American diplomats. Congress, just starting to recognize the nation's role as a world power, nonetheless had to be talked into posting ambassadors and sent them only to leading European and three Latin American nations. The first full ambassador from another country to present credentials to a president was Sir Julian Pauncefote of Great Britain, who beat the French ambassador to Grover Cleveland's White House by a single day. His was also the first government to buy or build a residence for its Washington representative—a brick house on Connecticut Avenue. "It is a hideous object outside," wrote *The Illustrated American* magazine, "but, like many other houses, and even individuals, the inner house is beautiful."

It would be wrong to say that our rambunctious new democracy did not envision itself as a diplomatic destination. The excitable dreamer who laid out the Plan of Washington, the Frenchman Pierre-Charles L'Enfant, pictured a "vast esplanade," worthy of Versailles, to be cleared from the Potomac thicket and along which "all such sort of places as may be attractive to the learned and afford diversion to the idle" might be located. Foreign legations were chief among this "sort of places." Instead, governments kept their distance from what was a pestiferous, brambly eyesore, and the Mall became a jumble of storehouses and railroad sheds before it was rehabilitated in the "City Beautiful" movement that swept the nation following the 1893 Chicago world's fair.

The first envoy to American shores was Conrad Alexander Gérad, who was appointed "minister plenipotentiary" in 1778—a year after France became the first nation to recognize the independence of Britain's 13 colonies, even though the war for freedom was still raging. Soon after the new United States settled upon the bumptious capital upstream from President George Washington's Mount Vernon home, the government sent notices to France, England, Spain, Portugal, and the Netherlands that it would be pleased to provide convenient sites along L'Enfant's proposed esplanade on which to "accommodate you agreeably." There were no takers. The foreign ministers who had dared take up residence in this callow country had found tolerable comfort in Philadelphia and saw no advantage to moving. When the relocation became official, the French minister asked for and was granted indefinite home leave in preference to a barbarous assignment in a miasmal bog.

In 1800, a week before President and Mrs. John Adams arrived to take up residence in the White House, Britain's George Hammond moved to town. So repulsed was he that he, too, soon sailed away, leaving the mission in the hands of an unfortunate chargé d'affaires. For almost a year after John and Abigail Adams set up housekeeping, only the Spanish minister, Llosa Ojeda, listed a Washington address, and he found excuses to spend most of his tour in Philadelphia and New York.

The city's first Embassy Row was actually a single abode—Decatur House on Lafayette Square, now a property of the National Trust for Historic Preservation. Designed by Benjamin Latrobe, who worked on both the Capitol and the White House, it was owned by Admiral Stephen Decatur until his death in a duel. His widow then rented out rooms to the representatives of various nations. Baron de Tuyll, the minister from imperial Russia, was Mrs. Decatur's bête noire. According to an article by the *Washington Post*'s Sarah Booth Conroy, written in 1976, "He built a greenhouse which caused her insurance to be canceled, and one of his servants tried to bill her for furniture he bought."

For the better part of a century, Washington was universally maligned as a hardship post, on the order of Rangoon or Timbuktu, with pay differentials to match. (It would remain a hardship post for black African diplomats well into the 20th century, as they sought equitable treatment in a segregated city.) In the earliest days of the capital, only the low in rank or the high in disfavor spent the summer in town. The Dutch ambassador arrived in 1801 but, according to Hope Ridings Miller in *Embassy Row,* "left the following year, complaining about the rigors of living in a frontier country." It would be 13 years before the Dutch bothered to send a replacement.

Miller tells the story of Sir Charles Bagot, the first British minister after the War of 1812, who had been counseled before arriving, "The problem confronting you is not so much what you can do in America, but how much you can bear." As it developed, he could bear little. "There is no enjoyment here," he wrote. "All I can hope to do is to prevent being unhappy, and that I shall manage by looking forward, or upward, or backward — any way but Yankeeward."

L'Enfant's magnificent radials were one thing on a map, quite another in reality for a century or more. Downtown streets were an odiferous morass when it rained, a choking slog of powdery dust when it did not. Nearly everything north of Florida Avenue — then fittingly called Boundary Street — was a "suburb" of verdant glens to which the gentry escaped by carriage and later streetcar to drink the purifying water, breathe agreeable air, check into sanitariums, or frolic at amusement parks. The part of the District of Columbia north of Boundary Street was not even in L'Enfant's original Washington City; it was called Washington County. When former Union general and U.S. Senator John Brooks Henderson built his three-story, red-sandstone "castle" at Florida Avenue and 16th Street in 1888, it pushed the limits of refined civilization north into the wilderness. Between 1906 and 1929, his wife (and widow as of 1913), Mary Foote Henderson, commissioned architect George Oakley Totten to construct a dozen palatial residences around nearby Meridian Hill, on which she sought to build a new presidential residence far grander than the White House. Failing that, she thought the Lincoln Memorial would look splendid nearby. Architects designed both, but Congress demurred. Finally she settled for a lovely park containing a memorial to President James Buchanan, a bronze statue of Dante, and an equestrian treatment of Joan of Arc. Wealthy industrialists, who had made their fortunes providing goods to the growing nation, bought or leased the grandiose Totten homes, such as the Pink Palace at 2600 16th Street, as second homes in Washington. Takers, too, were foreign governments, finally acknowledging the first-tier status of the United States. In the newspapers of the 1920s, 16th Street began to be known as Embassy Row.

Massachusetts Avenue, or rather the portion of Washington's longest thoroughfare from Scott Circle to Wisconsin Avenue, would wrest the title a decade later when the British built their new multimillion-dollar headquarters on "Massachusetts Avenue extended." Like 16th Street, the avenue had once been bucolic countryside, a favorite haunt of sports seekers. An 1809 city council "Act to Prevent Swine from Going at Large" set Massachusetts Avenue as the absolute boundary of citification. But after District of Columbia Governor Alexander "Boss" Shepherd graded and landscaped the avenue in the 1870s, it became a magnet for socialite expansion. Some of the city's first large-scale land speculators, the California Syndicate that included silver magnate and U.S. Senator William Stewart, gobbled up land west of Dupont Circle. Wealthy entrepreneurs, drawn to Washington to exert influence and further social ambitions, outdid one another in retaining architects and commissioning homes. The gas lamps of Massachusetts Avenue and Kalorama Heights mansions burned long into the night as the elite took turns celebrating their good fortune. When that fortune faded for many in the Great Depression—and when Uncle Sam began collecting income taxes—many of the barons of business left their drafty in-town mansions for less expensive, secluded homes in pastoral Maryland and Virginia. Soon the nouveau riche were establishing a beachhead on the avenue with smaller-scale places of their own; some of Embassy Row's great homes fell before the wrecker's crane, and others were converted to apartments or clubs. But several estates moved into the hands of foreign legations, which had been looking for fashionable elbow room and could afford to keep mansions out of the clutches of both subdividers and "revenuers," because they could not be taxed.

As the world's roster of countries raced past 100 and Washington's prestige as the capital of the free world soared, embassies of every size, resource, and geopolitical persuasion clustered as close to the old Embassy Row as their budgets would allow. Surprisingly, almost no diplomatic missions were located in now-fashionable Georgetown, which was considered a long haul from the White House and was somewhat seedy around the edges until the New Deal. A few embassies ventured farther afield, some into the business section of town but more than a few, illegally, into residential neighborhoods, to the consternation of inhabitants. Washington had become a plum rather than a hardship assignment. "A stay in Washington is considered very precipitous [sic] for our future career," Japanese embassy attaché Hiroaki Fujii told the *Washington Post* in 1979. After a tour of the new Japanese ambassador's home in 1978, the *Post*'s Conroy noted, "In Washington, embassies are our modern-day palaces, marble manifestations of the way the nations of the world wish to present themselves to other countries." So insatiable has been the diplomatic community's search for office space that the U.S. State Department publishes a fancy manual on acquiring foreign missions. It is shaped like an elongated U.S. passport, complete with a fake-leather cover and embossed State Department seal.

It was not until the 1950s that the first woman envoy arrived in Washington—Madame Vijaya Lakshmi Pandit, India's ambassador and sister of the then prime minister, Jawaharlal Nehru—and not until 1970 that the Executive Protective Service, the uniformed arm of the Secret

A baroque-style wood organ is built into the wall of the Indonesian embassy's music room, whose coffered ceiling is divided by dark beams into gilded ornamental panels.

15

Service, began patrolling diplomatic buildings. These measures were undertaken in response to increasingly combative demonstrations whose targets fluctuated with world events. Embassies of South Africa, the Soviet Union, Iran, Israel, Nicaragua, South Korea, and South Vietnam have been frequent objectives of protesters over the years. In 1988 the U.S. Supreme Court struck down a District of Columbia ban on demonstrations within 500 feet of an embassy, ruling that it violated the First Amendment right of free speech. The presence of Executive Protective Service guards also cut reported crime at embassies, which had included burglaries, stolen limousines, and several bombings. One crime that was planned but never happened: a proposal by the National Security Agency in the early 1970s to break into foreign embassies to steal their spy codes; Federal Bureau of Investigation Director J. Edgar Hoover nixed the idea "because of the risk," according to top-secret documents leaked to the press.

Many Washingtonians argue that the spread of embassies and chanceries—with their antenna nests, fleets of cars with diplomatic plates, claims on parking spaces, and renovations that turn lofty old mansions into office complexes—has been a blot on city neighborhoods. As early as 1945, *Nation's Business* estimated that 40,000 representatives were crowding into Washington, doing the work of foreign governments. By 1983 the city's 145 foreign missions and 23 international organizations owned 375 separate facilities around the city. In the early 1960s Congress and the city tried to slip a discrete chancery zone into Chevy Chase; howling neighbors' phone calls helped kill the scheme. Senator J. William Fulbright, who owned a house in the Sheridan-Kalorama section of the city, fielded numerous complaints about chancery sprawl, and Congress in the mid-1960s passed what became known as the Fulbright Amendment, restricting the expansion of new diplomatic facilities to high-density commercial or "mixed-use" zones.

In 1977 the National Capital Planning Commission published a comprehensive plan for missions and international agencies, and a year later Congress established a separate Office of Foreign Missions in the Department of State, in part to keep a rein on the skimble-skamble growth of chanceries. The planning commission went so far as to draw up blueprints for a chancery enclave near George Washington University Hospital in the Foggy Bottom section of the district, but congressional intervention once again scuttled the plan. The chancery-glut issue was finally somewhat ameliorated in the 1980s with the creation of an imposing International Center on 22 acres of federal land at the old National Bureau of Standards site at Connecticut Avenue and Van Ness Street uptown. By the early 1990s the chanceries of Austria, Bahrain, Ghana, Israel, Jordan, and Kuwait had located there. At the same time, construction began (and most likely will continue through much of the decade) on the last piece of the downtown Federal Triangle, the International Cultural and Trade Center, in what had been the Triangle's Great Plaza. The ICTC, the second largest federal building in the United States (after the Pentagon), was designed in part to accommodate foreign trade and cultural offices.

Embassies have come, gone, and sometimes come again. Few who worked diplomatic Washington in 1941 could forget the sight of smoke rising from the chimney of the German embassy, where the fine ashes of secret papers were rising skyward as the embassy prepared to close. "I must leave my horse, Kitty-Charr," the German ambassador's wife, Frau Annelsie Thomsen, regretfully told the *Washington Post*. "Also, I hate to leave all my little pets—I have 86 of them—squirrels, flying squirrels and birds. What will they do when I am not here to feed them?" She vowed to return after the war to renew friendships. "I wish all of you a merry, merry Christmas. Goodby."

The conduct of embassy affairs isn't all that upsets some locals' sensibilities. So does the off-the-job behavior of the diplomatic entourage. In 1990, for instance, a moonlighting Kuwait embassy messenger, stopped by metropolitan police, had to be reminded that delivering pizza in a car bearing embassy plates was out of diplomatic bounds. Over the years, higher-ranking envoys have also found themselves in embarrassing scrapes, including shoplifting incidents and auto accidents, from which only diplomatic immunity saved them. In 1962 the *Washington Star* even editorialized about the "disgraceful performance" of a Belgian air attaché, Colonel Maurice Schwarz, who had rammed another vehicle with his car, inflicting $500 in damage. "It is gratifying," wrote the *Star,* "that the State Department has taken special note of the affair, is investigating the circumstances, and has reminded all foreign diplomats that the shield of immunity is not broad enough to relieve them of responsibility to respect local laws and the rights of others. . . . It would be well to keep an eye on Colonel Schwarz in the future. If there is a repetition of anything of this sort he should be shipped home in a hurry." Straightening out such peccadilloes is a part of the turf of an entire State Department bureaucracy, the Office of Protocol.

The Spanish embassy was one of a dozen villas designed by architect George Oakley Totten as part of Mary Foote Henderson's plan for a grand diplomatic neighborhood carved from the 16th Street wilderness.

Today as always, the meat and potatoes of embassies' work involves assisting their nationals, issuing visas, dispensing business and travel information, representing their nations to the president and his officers, and conducting carefully choreographed exchanges among themselves. Statesmanlike tedium is the price the representative to Washington pays, but there is a most satisfactory trade-off. As Thomas Bailey pointed out in the 1940 *History of the American People,* the business of diplomacy is entertainment, "just as it is of the traveling salesman. The more people the ambassador ingratiates himself with, the better he can do his job. Many an important bit of information is dropped over the fourth cocktail. . . . Cynics have defined a diplomat as an 'honest man sent to lie abroad for his country.' He might perhaps better be defined as 'a man sent abroad to dine for his country,' sometimes on stewed cat."

Eric Sevareid and Robert A. Smith, in their 1965 book, *Washington: Magnificent Capital,* called diplomats "Washington's cosmopolitan night people": "With spidery unobtrusiveness, they form invisible webs of personal contacts, spinning gossamer strands of goodwill with a handshake, an embrace, an exchange of pleasantries, a whispered confidence, a raised glass, ingratiating themselves throughout the diplomatic, military, and political communities, snaring choice morsels of intelligence for the home office."

In this convivial milieu, especially during the social season from November through February, balancing a guest list becomes an art form, phrasing a toast or choosing a wine a tour de force. Indeed, the raconteurial renown of some former ambassadors is still remembered. So esteemed was one dean of the corps, the Frenchman Jules Jusserand, who regaled Washington from 1902 to 1925, that a plaque commemorating his service, presented at his farewell dinner, was placed in Rock Creek Park.

Balls, receptions, and trips past Washington's greatest groaning boards are standard diplomatic activities. First among equals on the social circuit are Holland's Tulip Festival, Sweden's Santa Lucia Christmas repast, national independence day celebrations at numerous embassies, strawberries and cream and toasts to the queen's birthday at the British embassy, Columbus Day festivities, and the French commemoration of Bastille Day. The most elegant of all diplomatic do's is the annual White House reception, first made glamorous by John and Jacqueline Kennedy.

But many embassy events serve a nobler purpose than the displaying of new finery. Harking back to World War II "Bundles for Britain" soirees and French Red Cross receptions are the annual embassy tours, which give the inquisitive public a peek inside these glamorous quarters, with admission fees going to various charities. One of the first tours, in the early 1940s, benefited the Washington Home for the Incurables, but the most enduring has been a springtime fixture of Goodwill Industries. The Goodwill Guild's first affair, in 1947, drew 500 ladies in hats and gloves and netted Goodwill $800; Bess Truman was a hostess for the concluding tea. Now the Goodwill Embassy Tour and Gala cut off ticket sales at 3,000.

So intense was one Washingtonian's curiosity about the elusive workings of an embassy that she wrote to *Washington Daily News* columnist Evelyn Peyton Gordon in 1947, asking how she might get invited to a reception. "It's not such a difficult problem, my dear lady," replied Gordon, who advised her to get some "visiting cards" correctly engraved, "wear your best clothes and gloves," and set forth, leaving cards at chosen residences. "If the envoy has a wife, two cards should be left — a Mr. and Mrs. card for the diplomat and his wife, and a Mr. card for the envoy. A woman never calls on a man. An unmarried man leaves

Tiles from Puebla, Mexico, laid in 1937 at the Mexican Cultural Institute, depict the shields of the Mexican states and a view of the ancient cities of Popocatepetl and Ixtacihvatt.

two of his cards, and a single woman leaves one card for the madame. Unfortunately an unmarried woman can not call on a bachelor envoy." *Cosmopolitan* magazine reported the outrage, in 1901, that followed the arrival at the Mexican embassy of a mother with "a brood of dirty children." They barged into the ballroom, and after settling the youngsters on a French-upholstered divan, the woman "proceeded to the dining-room and helped herself to enough cake to satisfy the ravenous youngsters. It is hardly to be wondered at, therefore, that to give a public entertainment is not regarded as a pleasure by the foreign Embassies, and the decline of this form of function has been very rapid." Public tours of embassies are indeed rare today, more for reasons of security than of propriety.

An article published in 1958 in *Better Homes and Gardens* magazine divulged the strict schedule governing an ambassador's formal dinners: "Guests are invited for 8 p.m., and are expected to be no more than five minutes late. At 10:45 p.m., the ranking guest is supposed to leave, whereupon everybody else may then leave if they like. If it is an extremely good party, sometimes the ranking guest will depart, take a walk around the block, and return. This ploy, it seems, automatically cancels all protocol about protocol."

The sashaying side to diplomacy, the elegant repasts with starchy conventions and vacuous conversations have provoked the sharpest barbs. From the late United Nations ambassador and presidential candidate Adlai Stevenson: "A diplomat's life is made up of three ingredients: protocol, Geritol, and alcohol." Actor Peter Ustinov: "A diplomat these days is nothing but a headwaiter who's allowed to sit down occasionally." And the late Italian writer and diplomat Daniele Vare: "Diplomacy is the art of letting someone else have your way."

In 1984 novelist Sondra Gotlieb, wife of the then Canadian ambassador, wrote in the *Washington Post* about the visit of "Popsie Tribble," who "drops in every six weeks or so to tell me how to conduct my life in Washington." Popsie brought a list of do's (hire a butler who can announce the guests by their right names) and don'ts (avoid pregnant maids). Popsie and Sondra looked in on the kitchen and found the new Bulgarian chef with "a tumbler in one hand while he basted some ducks with the other.

"Popsie said loudly, 'I think you should fire him.'

"'Don't you think I should wait till after dinner?' I whispered. 'There are thirty people coming this evening.'

"'Maybe that's wise,' she agreed, and we went upstairs."

In 1956 *Washington Star* society columnist Betty Beale listed some of the pet peeves of "party-trotting women" who frequented the embassy scene. The greatest affront of all: coat-checkers' "cozy little custom of leaving a dish out with coins in it in hopes of getting more. To have to pay to get your own garments back at a private party is certainly the ne plus ultra of the bottom drawer!"

In 1973 *Washington Post* writer Henry Mitchell devoted some space to a comparison of canapés at various embassy affairs. He described the "peculiarly excellent" Swedish meatballs at the Dutch embassy and strawberries "at their peak" at the Belgian embassy during the daffodil season, but "mealy and often hollow" at the Japanese embassy. "But things even out," he wrote. "The Japanese melon balls were great." Had Mitchell made the circuit several decades earlier, during the Great Depression, he'd have been caustic indeed. So grim was the international stock and banking crisis that cocktails were served without olives, liquor was rationed, and sea water substituted for gin. Many envoys served at nominal wages or without pay for the duration.

Until the 1980s, the typical society-page coverage of an embassy event consisted of an opening paragraph describing the time, place, and nature of the affair, followed by several columns listing each and every guest and what he—and especially she—wore. Every word was flattering, at least at first read. A typical entry was Hazel Markel's notation in a 1951 issue of *The Diplomat:* "Mme. Henri Bonnet receiving for famed Gen. Jean de Lattre de Tassigny, wearing Christian Dior's stunning emerald-toned taffeta, a low cut bodice, a side-swept crinolined skirt and yards on yards of dotted white chiffon stole." The columnists' colleagues in the feature section were not always so saccharine.

Early on, the typical ambassador's attire sported epaulets and medals; some men turned down important foreign posts because they could not keep up appearances. Fashion plates in the diplomatic corps wore hussar capes, Turkish fezzes, diamond-encrusted turbans, Oriental silks, a variety of Knights Templar uniforms, and, reported *Cosmopolitan* in 1901, coats with "frogs and slashes" and "astrakhan-trimmed chapeaux with black feather tufts." It was during the presidency of Andrew Jackson, who ran with a coonskin-cap crowd, that "the simple dress of an American citizen," occasionally augmented by a sword, would be fine for Washington's diplomatic gentlemen. Years later, a standard business suit by day and dinner jacket by night became the uniform. Titled noblemen, who once dominated Washington diplomacy, were a rarity by 1935, when only 19 of 431 envoys were to the manner born. One, however, the British ambassador, Sir Ronald Lindsay, had a string of 12 honorary initials (P.C., G.C.M.G., K.C.B., C.V.O.) trailing after his name.

The duties of these envoys have rarely been described as arduous. "There is work enough to keep the blood from stagnating in most houses, perhaps," wrote the *Star* in 1928, "but when breakfast has been eaten, the diplomat has before him a pleasant afternoon and evening."

Making a good impression and unraveling misunderstandings are two of the envoy's responsibilities. "Being an ambassador these days is a bit like being an airline stewardess," Henry Catto, then U.S. ambassador to the Court of St. James and later director of the United States Information Agency, told *Washingtonian* magazine in 1991. "You serve many meals, and you clean up minor messes." Forty years earlier, writer Robley D. Stevens pointed out in an article on embassy public relations in *The Diplomat,* "[The ambassador] must win the confidence of the American people. . . . He should talk a 'plain' language—discuss the affairs of his country as related to the American scene without hesitancy. Nothing will win Americans more quickly than the knowledge that the 'man at the top' is a 'regular fellow' and that he also has problems."

The Diplomat was a chichi publication produced from 1941 to 1966, based in Washington but catering to the gentility on the go worldwide. Washington's embassies themselves got scant treatment, but the comings and goings of their ambassadors were lavishly covered. "The great 'Whispering Gallery' that is our nation's capital reverberates with rumors of what goes on in the Inner Circle and speculations as to Who will be Who here after November," wrote a columnist in 1964. *The Diplomat's* regular features, tucked amid advertising for furriers, cruise lines, violin studios, and Cadillac dealerships, included seasonal updates from the Hamptons, Bermuda, Nassau, and Palm Beach. Debs from Dallas to Philadelphia got coverage. The diplomatic set read about "leg loveliness for summer," "male plumage," and "matching lips and nails." Regular columns included "Confessions of a Grand Duke" and "Celebrities at Play."

In its December 1953 tip on protocol, *The Diplomat* informed the haut monde how to address an ambassador properly: "'His excellency' is the complimentary title. . . . Personal titles, such as 'Baron,' 'Count,' 'Jonkheer,' etc., which are indications of rank or intimately associated with certain foreign names, are to be added."

Such flowery discourse gets shorter shrift today. "Society" columns of newspapers have given way to "Style" or "Living" sections that glorify more rock musicians and film stars than debutantes. Hope Ridings Miller, who was the *Washington Post* society editor for seven years, once, in a blue moment, wrote a column titled "Farewell to Society." "What's killed it," she told the authors of this book, "is that they [the society set] can't get publicity any more. That's important to the 'climbers,' and it's important to the embassies, in order to justify their 'representational funds,' the funds for entertainment. They still give parties; they're just not written up as much. But, believe me, next to an invitation to the White House, an embassy invitation still rates."

Nowadays, issues far graver than who sits to the right of the host occupy the ambassador posted to Washington. Complexities of trade, long-simmering ethnic resentments inside and among nations, even overnight changes in ideology have encumbered the diplomat's job. Who could have foreseen the day when delirious mobs would topple statues of Lenin and snip the hammer and sickle from national flags? Even with such dizzying complications, however, when the sun dips below the Potomac and the first drinks are served or the first dance announced, the magic of cultivated conversation, well-bred courtliness, and exquisite fashion still shimmers inside these residences. It is into this unflappable world that *Embassies of Washington* invites you.

The Red Living Room at the Spanish ambassador's residence showcases a rug created at the Real Fabrica de Tapices in Madrid. Following pages: The Belgian ambassador's house is a faithful reproduction of the Hôtel de Charolais in Paris.

RESIDENCE OF THE AMBASSADOR OF BELGIUM

Baker's Acres

2300 Foxhall Road, Northwest

Horace Trumbauer, Architect

1931

Up to 30 guests can enjoy legendary cuisine in the Belgian ambassador's dining room. The gold-trimmed white china bears the Belgian seal; the crystal is Val St. Lambert.

IN 1931 THE *WASHINGTON DAILY NEWS* REPORTED that "one of the most widely known figures in society, both in America and in Europe" was about to build a $310,000 home to occupy "the entire 2300 block of Foxhall Road nw." That dapper figure was Raymond T. Baker, a onetime Nevada gold prospector, prison warden, and Reno bank president who had served as private secretary to the U.S. ambassador to Russia and as Woodrow Wilson's secretary of the Mint. His new house rose on Baker's Acres, so dubbed, in part, because it covered 13 (a baker's dozen) acres.

The limestone château, which a *Washington Star* reviewer would call "a petit palais at the edge of the woods," is an accurate reproduction of the Hôtel de Charolais in Paris. Its specifications, remarkable for the time, included a cold-storage room for rugs and furs, a refrigeration room for cut flowers, and a storage chamber specially designed to closet bottled water. Crystal chandeliers, Aubusson carpets, parquet floors, and carved paneling were imported from France. Philadelphia architect Horace Trumbauer, whose work included that city's Ritz-Carlton Hotel, paid special attention to the wide rear terrace, which offers a vista of the Virginia countryside across the Potomac River. In the opposite direction, across Foxhall Road, was another expanse of woods soon to be filled by a second legendary estate, on which storied Washington hostess and philanthropist Gwendolyn Cafritz would site her 15,000-square-foot Art Moderne home.

The Bakers' neighbor down the road was Mrs. J. Borden Harriman, whose Terrace Heights estate had been built two years earlier. According to Hope Ridings Miller in *The Great Houses of Washington*, Daisy Harriman and Delphine Baker were fast friends and fellow Democratic Party shakers, but their friendship did not deter Daisy Harriman from suing the Bakers for $15,000 when workers clearing Baker's Acres dumped 15 tons of dirt onto Harriman land. The parties quietly settled out of court.

Baker, whom an obituary called "a man with an attractive personality, with a natural gift for making friends among all sorts of people," married well, first to Margaret Emerson, heiress to the Bromo-Seltzer fortune, then to Delphine Dodge Cromwell of the Detroit automobile family. (The first Mrs. Baker took her divorce in stride, proceeding to marry Alfred Gwynne Vanderbilt.) Baker died in the house within four years of its christening.

The French Renaissance home remained a hub of social gaiety, however. It was leased by Dwight F. Davis, who had served as secretary of war, and then by the queen of Palm Beach Society, Mrs. Edward T. Stotesbury. According to Hope Miller, one of Mrs. Stotesbury's most memorable soirees was set for December 7, 1941, a few hours "after the jaw-shivering news of Pearl Harbor hit Washington. Foreign emissaries, high State Department officials, and enough members of the House and Senate to pass a congressional bill were in the distressed throng that milled through the mansion's salons that evening."

In 1945 the Baker house, as it was still known, was sold to the Belgian government, which was desperately seeking larger embassy

quarters. Belgian war-supply efforts had been conducted out of rooms at the old embassy on Massachusetts Avenue.

But the entertainment schedule at Baker's Acres hardly skipped a beat. Baron Robert Silvercruys and his successor, Baron Louis M. Scheyven, were both connoisseurs of decorative arts. Baron Scheyven, who had held diplomatic posts throughout the world, installed silver plates from Egypt, icons from Russia and Germany, ivory bulls from China, and a wooden madonna and infant from his homeland. The embassy library—a replica of the one presented by the late J. Pierpont

Morgan to the Metropolitan Museum of Art in New York—seated 50 and was dominated by a flamboyant scarlet phoenix, emblem of the Chinese empress. The wife of a French ambassador to the United States remarked that the Louis XVI salon was "the most beautiful room in Washington."

Baron Scheyven, a gourmet, was fond of recalling that he "learned something about food" when he steamed to China as a galley boy on a Pacific liner. One of his sumptuous repasts is recalled in *Embassy Row* as meeting "the last word in excellence," attesting to the adage "The French cuisine is good; the Belgian is divine." It should be noted, however, that the Belgian national meat dish is biftek, which the book *Diplomatic Dishes* says is "usually prepared with ox, calf, pig, or horse."

On November 15, 1974, Ambassador Willy Van Cauwenberg got a chuckle from the 750 guests at his first big reception on "the occasion of The King's Day." It turned out not to be King Baudouin's birthday, which was September 7, nor the Belgians' national day, which is July 21. An embassy official interpolated that it must be "St. Leopold's Day," safe in the knowledge that there had been three King Leopolds. But a prankish guest quick-checked a history book and found no correlation with any of the Leopolds. By evening's end, the invitees had settled on a celebration of the birthday of St. Albert, predecessor to one of the Leopolds.

The Belgians also once earned a titter when an embassy secretary maintained, unsuccessfully, that her pet ocelots Sabu and Elizabeth had diplomatic immunity and should not be confiscated.

But most of the attention focuses on the graceful château itself and its contents. The Hauteville marble floor and post-impressionist Taf Wallet paintings in the entrance hall, the replica of a library of natural-finished oak designed by Georges Hoentschel, drawing-room tapestries woven after cartoons by the Belgian painter Edgard Tytgat, and hand-made Belgian crystal throughout the house are among the city's most remarkable furnishings.

Lush gardens, once the pride of Delphine Dodge Baker, second wife of the director of the U.S. Mint, grace the Belgian ambassador's home. A sunny informal Garden Room opens onto it.

THE GLOBE-TROTTING DAUGHTER OF THE FOUNDER
of the *Chicago Tribune,* married to the former U.S. ambassador to Austria-
Hungary, then Russia, and then France, could afford a fancy address for
the couple's new home in Washington. Katherine Medill McCormick
bought an imposing triangular corner of Pretty Prospect along Massachusetts Avenue, part of the Rock of Dumbarton property north of
Georgetown, and hired John Russell Pope to create a new home for her
and her husband, Robert, that would provide a proper setting for the
collection of exquisite furnishings the McCormicks had acquired in their
far-ranging travels. Pope—the man destined to become one of America's
great Classical Revival architects—would later design three of Washington's most imposing structures: the National Gallery of Art, the National Archives building, and the Jefferson Memorial. He was already
thinking big when he went to work on the McCormick mansion.

     Katherine's husband, "Colonel" Robert McCormick—the isola-
tionist publisher of the *Tribune* and the *Washington Times-Herald*—died in
1919, and five years later Mrs. McCormick deeded the house and land
(for $10) and the "furniture, pictures, draperies, rugs, tapestries, bric-a-
brac, objects of art, and household furnishings of every kind" (for another $10) to her son, U.S. Senator Medill McCormick. Yet Mother Mc-
Cormick, and not the senator, kept the house as a Washington address
when she was not back in Chicago or avidly touring abroad; indeed, she
would die in a hotel in Versailles. Her son, the senator, died in 1925, and
his widow, Ruth (herself the daughter of Senator Mark Hanna), made
a run for his seat; she won the Republican nomination but lost the elec-
tion. At Katherine McCormick's death in 1931, title to the Massachusetts
Avenue mansion reverted to her daughter-in-law. Ruth also inherited
Katherine's furs and laces. A *New York Times* article about Katherine Mc-
Cormick's estate noted that "Mrs. McCormick made it clear in her will
that all the contents of her house at 3000 Massachusetts Avenue were
the property of her son, Medill McCormick, and are now the property
of Mrs. Simms." "Mrs. Simms" was Ruth McCormick Simms, who had
married New Mexico Congressman Albert G. Simms a year after her
mother-in-law's death. In 1934 the Simmses sold the mansion to "The
United States of Brazil" for $200,000, following what a Brazilian publi-
cation called "intense negotiations." Albert and Ruth then moved back
to Illinois—turf of the Medills and McCormicks—where Ruth became
publisher of two newspapers in Rockford.

     With the purchase of the McCormick house, Brazil became the
second nation, after Great Britain, to locate an embassy on Massachusetts Avenue. The Brazilians modified the downstairs, turning the
library into a state dining room and eliminating several service rooms.
A year later, on land they bought next door along Whitehaven Street
from the McCormick estate for another $50,000, they erected a
chancery—replaced by a modern structure in 1971.

     A slick, 46-page brochure published by the embassy in 1986,
somewhat belatedly marking the 50th anniversary of its government's
purchase of the McCormick house, recalls that embassy affairs had previously been conducted in a variety of cramped locations in northwest

RESIDENCE OF THE
AMBASSADOR OF BRAZIL
McCormick House
3000 Massachusetts Avenue, Northwest
John Russell Pope, Architect
1910

RESIDENCE AND STAFF OFFICES OF THE AMBASSADOR OF GREECE

Jennings House

2221 Massachusetts Avenue, Northwest

George Oakley Totten, Jr., Architect

═══ 1906 ═══

THERE WAS SOMETHING ABOUT WASHINGTON— proximity to power, in no small measure—that was a magnet for men who made millions in mining. John Hays Hammond, W. W. Lawrence, and Tom Walsh all built monumental homes in Washington in the early years of this century. And so did Hennen Jennings, a Kentucky-born, Harvard-educated engineer and pal of Hammond's, who joined the millionaires' club by consulting to British gold-mining interests in South Africa and Venezuela. His house at Sheridan Circle years later became an embassy (Greece), as did those of Hammond (France), Lawrence (Portugal), and Walsh (Indonesia). Jennings commissioned George Oakley Totten, Jr., to design the house. Totten would become a preferred architect of wealthy Washingtonians and designed several other residences around Sheridan Circle (one of which, a couple of doors up the avenue, is also owned and used by the Greeks).

Sheridan Circle had been close to the outer reaches of Massachusetts Avenue until it was extended to Observatory Circle in the 1870s. It was a fancy, almost-suburban address for Hennen and Mary Jennings, and they entertained with verve and splendor. Mary, herself a mining magnate's daughter who had seen the arrival of the Pony Express near her home in California, would, with Hennen, live through the Boer War in South Africa, taste Victorian society in London, and make the social scene in New York. She was also a renowned philanthropist—earning the French Médaille de Reconnaissance for her work on behalf of the American branch of the Fatherless Children of France—and a tireless worker for the Washington Home for the Incurables. After her husband's death in 1920, Mary Jennings remained in the house until she rented it to the Greek government in 1935. Two years later a wealthy Greek-American business executive, William Helis, bought it and donated it to his native country.

Washington Daily News reporter George Abell was on hand for the house's regal housewarming as the Greek legation:

Everybody came crowding to the new legation . . . to drink champagne and Scotch, to gossip and to marvel. There might have been a jam except that the house is so huge.

"Wonderful," enthused the guests.

"This coffee ice cream is the best I've ever tasted."

"How do they do it?" whispered an Ambassador to a colleague.

"Everywhere—from the rose-colored drawing room to a cozy little corner, full of cigaret smoke and syphons, near the buffet—rose a clamor of praise."

The "beautiful, the bizarre, the banal" were on hand, Abell continued. "Adolf Hitler's special representative, tall, blond Herbert Scholtz, and his handsome wife, arrived at the same time. Bald and benevolent Dr. Ernst Meyer [German] first secretary, came in whistling 'Dei Wacht am Rhein' and swinging a malacca walking stick."

Three years later, the Greek ambassador, Demetrios Sicilianos, spoke about the house—and Greek cooking—with *Washington Times-Herald* reporter Carol Frink. "It always seems strange to me that when this house was built, some 30 years ago or so, there was no possible way

nament culled with skillful abandon from the Beaux Arts book of historical styles."

Affording it was not a problem. "Each morning, we Walshes arose richer than we had gone to bed," Evalyn would later write in her autobiography, *Father Struck It Rich.*

The house has a distinctive entryway rising three stories to a stained-glass, domed ceiling with a Y-shaped central staircase reminiscent of an ocean liner's, eight fireplaces, a ballroom and theater (for little "Vin," who played at acting), and bathtubs that, according to a *Washington Star* article in 1957, are "small swimming pools." The dining room is a replica of King Leopold's.

The king never made it to Washington, but his nephew, King Albert, and Queen Elizabeth did in 1919, nine years after Tom Walsh's death. Just as the Belgian royalty was arriving, President Woodrow Wilson suffered a stroke, and the White House was taken out of the entertainment loop. Mrs. Walsh volunteered her mansion for the state dinner, yielding the host's role to Vice President and Mrs. Thomas Riley Marshall. For the occasion, everything possible was Walsh gold, from the chrysanthemums and candelabra to the table service forged from Camp Bird ore.

Tom Walsh had got in his share of entertaining before he died. Even when he and Carrie dined alone, their organist, Dr. Harry Wheaton Howard of St. Aloysius Church, on yearly retainer, serenaded on the house's magnificent baroque organ. In *Father Struck It Rich,* Evalyn Walsh McLean recalled poking holes in a canvas screen that looked into a dining room and joining her brother, Vinson, in bombing her father's guests, including President William Howard Taft, with projectiles from a bean shooter. At a ball and cotillion soon after the house was opened in 1903, the Walshes welcomed Alice Roosevelt, daughter of President Theodore Roosevelt. Evalyn, deemed too young at 17, was not invited and pouted in her room. According to Helena McCartha, the *Evening Star*'s society editor, favors included lace fans with tortoise-shell handles for the girls and gold (not gold-colored) pencils for the men. "Poke bonnets and peasant headgear, cuff and handkerchief boxes, handbags and purses were other pretty and useful gifts," she reported. At another bash, 325 guests consumed 480 quarts of champagne, 288 fifths of scotch, 40 gallons of beer, and 36 bottles of liqueur. "It really is a palace that expresses dreams my father and mother had when they were poor in Colorado," she wrote in *Father Struck It Rich.* "This should not give rise to any notion they were sadly 'nouveau' as that term is used to label people outside of society trying to get in. We were in; make no mistake about it. . . ." Recalling the heydays of the mansion, she added, "How the money went!"

In 1905 Vinson was killed, and Evalyn badly injured, when Vin drove Evalyn's Mercedes off a bridge in Newport, R.I. A bathroom at "2020"—the Walshes' unpretentious name for their home—was turned into an operating room for Evalyn's hip surgery; she would wear a silver plate in her hip for the rest of her life. She also developed a morphine habit and wrote in her book about walking the cavernous house, night after night, loving this grand home even more.

In 1908 Evalyn and Edward Beale McLean, whose father owned the *Washington Post* and the *Cincinnati Enquirer,* eloped, but they were certainly not disinherited. After the death of Edward's father, they were living in their own urban paradise, the "Friendship" estate (site of today's McLean Gardens apartments) on Wisconsin Avenue, where their breakfasts on New Year's Day, Easter, and Thanksgiving became Washington traditions. They continued to drop in for soirees at their mother's mansion. Evalyn still kept many of her sables and silks in a top-floor room the size of a dress shop, and it was there in 1911 that the McLeans arranged to buy the Hope Diamond.

Inside the Walsh mansion, Evalyn's mother always busied herself with charitable endeavors. During World War I, she and her friends gathered up old clothes, turned the oak dining room into a sewing parlor, and fashioned garments for Belgian refugees. Once a week, she threw the house open to members of the service for music and dancing. The events became so popular that she had to issue admission cards to the "2020 Dancing Class."

The public-service tradition continued after Carrie Walsh's death in 1932. After standing empty for three years, the mansion was rented to the U.S. Resettlement Administration, whose mission was to provide suburban bungalows for city slum dwellers. Bureaucrats were observed having a fine time lunching on the grand staircase, typing letters in Mrs. Walsh's former boudoir, riding the gilded elevator, yanking on the servants' bell-cords, and dictating memos in front of the tapestried walls (wisely covered with cellophane to minimize staining). In 1937 the relocators moved out, their director admitting that placing a New Deal agency in such swanky quarters was unseemly and becoming a political millstone. More civil servants, from the U.S. Rural Electrification Administration, moved in for a time, but then the house fell empty again.

In 1940 there were press reports that the Walsh mansion would "go commercial," but instead Evalyn McLean and her mother's other trustees turned it over, rent free for 10 years, to the District of Columbia chapter of the Red Cross. In the house during World War II, Red Cross workers wrapped bandages—at the rate of 100,000 a month. At the time the lease expired in 1950, the Red Cross was using it as a center for educational services, and the Washington Workshop gave classes in sculpture, dancing, and art in the ballroom and other fourth-floor quarters.

The Republic of Indonesia, the nation of many islands—once called the Dutch East Indies—had won its independence in 1949 and

Evalyn Walsh McLean was a fancier of jewelry. A photograph from an *Evening Star* of the period shows her with a five-inch-high gold choker studded with diamonds. And the idea of owning the world's largest diamond intrigued her. The 44 ½-carat Hope Diamond was acquired from Cartier Frères of Paris for $154,000 ($40,000 down, the rest in three installments over three years). The *New York Times* reported that it would be worn by Evalyn McLean "as a head ornament arranged in a bandeau, the large stone being placed immediately in front with other diamonds of lesser size." Evalyn actually pawned the diamond a couple of times before selling it, in 1940, to New York jeweler Harry Winston, who donated it to the Smithsonian Institution.

Evalyn McLean would later insist the famous "curse" of the Hope Diamond had passed her by, but she did suffer a string of tragedies. In 1919 her son Vinson—the "hundred-million-dollar baby" who had slept in a crib made of gold, the gift of King Leopold—ran into traffic and was killed by a car. She and Edward were separated in 1930 and, three years later, he was declared insane, hospitalized, and died in 1941. "At intervals I get reports from a Maryland hospital concerning a patient there who has morbid preoccupations and lives in a state of mental exile," Evalyn wrote, "shut off even from himself. If he is addressed by his right name he grows excited and swears he is not McLean." Evalyn, who moved back to "2020," died in 1947.

was looking for suitable embassy quarters. In 1951 the Indonesians bought the Walsh mansion from Carrie Walsh's estate for $335,000, half a million dollars less (not even counting inflation) than Thomas Walsh had spent to build it 48 years earlier.

The Indonesians did not revive the mansion's elbow-bending party tradition; as Muslims, most Indonesians do not drink alcohol. But they did spend eight months and $75,000 to eradicate most of the vestiges of the palace's federal and institutional occupancy, replacing stained-glass panes in the entrance-hall ceiling, removing the termite-infested wooden floor in the basement and installing one of concrete, restoring Italian master paintings that had been damaged, stitching worn tapestries, and celebrating the Walshes' love of gold motifs where possible. At the embassy's opening reception in 1952, at which Ambassador Ali Sastroamidjojo presided, the 500 guests marveled at the gold brocade tapestry in the music room—and at Madame Sastroamidjojo's matching gold lace jacket.

Four years later, the *Washington Star*'s Selwa Roosevelt visited and found that "of the elaborate furnishings from the Walsh era nothing remains but a tiny white piano which once made happy music in the ballroom on the top floor. Now the piano is in the basement, looking a bit forlorn, with its keys discolored." In 1981 Sarah Booth Conroy toured the Indonesians' "warren of offices" and noted, "The house looks like a magnificent grande dame sent out to earn a living in a job to which her past life had not accustomed her."

The Indonesians added an exotic touch to the mansion with the installation of a *gamelan,* a 100-year-old collection of musical, chiefly percussion, instruments enjoyed by area students, embassy personnel, and guests at receptions, incorrectly described by the *Star* as "a pantry full of copper pots and pans." Visitors to those receptions still delight in hearing rumors that Tom Walsh had hidden a huge gold nugget in the house. One tale has it that the Indonesians, when they took over, found the treasure amid the flagstones of the front walkway (the Resettlement Administration workers and Red Cross volunteers somehow having stepped on it thousands of times without finding it).

But the legend is not apocryphal. In 1953 a Seton Hall professor who was a student of mining history—and of Thomas Walsh in particular—discovered a 12-by-15-inch slab of gold ore in the facing supporting the house's piazza. Lest Washingtonians descend with picks and jackhammers, he quickly pointed out that it takes a ton of such ore to yield $100 and that the artifact had no doubt been Tom Walsh's symbolic souvenir.

In 1982 the Indonesian government built a $1.3 million addition to the mansion—set back from Massachusetts Avenue as if in deference to the stately old building—which was designed by Architects Collaborative of Cambridge, Massachusetts. Several chancery functions moved there, with the grandest parts of the Walsh house thus made available for entertaining. Guests still stream through the door, passing under the Indonesian coat of arms symbolizing the nation's 1,300 islands. The motto upon it reads: "Unity through Diversity."

The Walshes' Louis XIV drawing room now holds the instruments of a traditional Indonesian gamelin orchestra, which once belonged to the Sultan of Jogjakhara, a royal court in Java.

RESIDENCE OF THE
AMBASSADOR OF ITALY

Villa Firenze

2800 Albemarle Street, Northwest

Russell Kluge, Architect

1927

*A majolica vase and
statue of a saint
rest atop a Louis XIV
table at the foot of
Villa Firenze's reception
room staircase.
Following pages:
The onetime home of
Colonel and Mrs.
Robert Guggenheim
has surprisingly
informal spaces such as
this enclosed sunroom.*

IF ANYONE WAS UNHAPPY TO LEARN THAT THE GOV-
ernment of Italy had purchased Villa Firenze with the idea of turning
its 59-room manor house into a residence for its ambassador in 1976, it
was the tax-collection office of the District of Columbia, for the property had carried the sixth-highest tax assessment in the city. The purchase price was $4,335,000.

Firenze's gray Tudor mansion, made of brick, wood, stucco, and
fieldstone—the stone quarried on the estate—was built in 1925 by
Blanche Estabrook Roebling O'Brien, widow of a member of the firm
that built the Brooklyn Bridge. Blanche O'Brien had a 60-foot-long
swimming pool built first; she and her friends picnicked around it as the
manor house rose and later twirled upon the wooden dance floor that
covered the pool.

In the 1930s Blanche O'Brien leased the estate to the government
of Hungary, which turned it into a popular diplomatic gathering place.
In 1941 it was sold to Colonel Robert Guggenheim (a Silver Star vet-
eran of World War I) and his wife, Rebecca "Polly" Guggenheim, who
had been residing on their oceangoing yacht, *Firenze,* on the Potomac
River when the U.S. Navy requested it for possible wartime service. Recalling another Tudor home in which he grew up—also named Firenze
after his mother, Florence (*Firenze* in Italian)—Guggenheim, heir to the
family copper fortune, promptly christened his new estate Firenze.

Colonel Guggenheim would briefly serve as President Eisen-
hower's ambassador to Portugal. After the colonel's death in 1959, Polly
and her second husband, John Logan, lived in the house. Logan had
founded a national association of food chains and had expanded its op-
erations overseas. He was also the longtime chairman of Washington's
Cherry Blossom Festival Ball. The Logans used Firenze for numerous
community functions, often as a setting for the charitable sale of art.
Polly also used the airy manor to show off her world-class collection of
glass. When the sale to the Italian government was announced and the
family was preparing to move furnishings to a winter home on St. Croix
and to a new estate on S Street, N.W., Polly Logan told the *Washington
Post,* "We'll have to have a garage sale . . . a six-car garage sale. Won't
that be fun?" When she left, she took stone lions that had stood beside
the garden terrace. "[They] go everywhere with me," she said. "I'm born
a Leo, and lions are my symbol."

At first, little about Villa Firenze or its grounds strike one as
Italian. From the back of the house, rolling hills and woods, part of the
city's Rock Creek Park, recall the Cotswold area of southwest England. The driveway off Albemarle Street passes the gardener's cottage,
painting studio, and garage. A second drive, off Broad Branch Road,
winds through a thick woods. The embassy's enormous oak front door
and its long heavy wrought-iron bell pull seem more appropriate for a
residence of Henry VIII. Inside, a spacious entryhall with a minstrel's
gallery, added by the Guggenheims, is paneled in pickled oak. The hall
includes a rotunda ceiling featuring signs of the zodiac in bas-relief.
Off the hall is one of the most unusual rooms in the house: the di-
minutive library where original owner Blanche O'Brien had installed

17th-century wood paneling taken from the study of British architect Christopher Wren, recreating the original study's exact dimensions.

While the architecture is derivative of English models, the furnishings are unmistakenly Italian, with pieces dating from the Baroque era. A 15th-century painting on wood of the madonna and child from the school of Sandro Botticelli and a carved wood statue of Catherine of Alessandria, a 14th-century saint, share space in the entrance hall. Some fabrics were woven at the Fortuny factory in Venice; 18th-century gold-inlaid mirrors come from Naples; crystal chandeliers and sconces hail from Murano, while decorative jugs come from the Capodimonte factory near Naples.

Villa Firenze is perfectly suited for entertaining (it has one of the largest dining rooms of any private home in the city). While a president of the United States rarely attends strictly social functions in diplomatic residences, President Ronald Reagan did attend a Columbus Day lunch here during his first administration. And the residence has hosted numerous celebrities throughout the years, including, for an awards dinner in 1989, tenor Luciano Pavarotti, writer Umberto Eco, and actress Sophia Loren, who on previous visits also had used the four-room suite upstairs during the tenure of Ambassador and Mrs. Rinaldo Petrignani.

This 39-room villa once was called "Estabrook," after its first owner, Blanche Estabrook Roebling O'Brien, who had the 60-foot outdoor pool built first so friends could loll and watch construction.

RESIDENCE OF THE
AMBASSADOR OF THE
IVORY COAST

Livingston's Vale

5111 Broad Branch Road, Northwest

1927

WHEN "WASH" WILLIAMS, OWNER OF WASHINGTON'S biggest Schlitz beer distributorship, and his wife in 1947 inspected the house they had heard was for sale at 5111 Broad Branch Road, they found more of a home than they bargained for. The fortresslike house that peers down on Rock Creek Park was sealed shut with boards, its interior caked in layers of dust, but what lay under the grime proved irresistible.

This place, where a whimsical intruder had drawn "Kilroy was here" in the dust, had been the home of eccentric world traveler Lily Livingston, who had died two years earlier, leaving a million-dollar estate including a horse farm in Virginia and a $1,000 bequest for the care of Pee Wee, her fox terrier. Lily's husband, George, a wealthy former New York public official, had built Livingston's Vale in 1927 on a part of the estate of contractor T. Franklin Schneider, who had built several of the Henderson 16th Street mansions that later became embassies.

Both the Williams family and the government of the Ivory Coast, which purchased the house as an ambassador's residence in 1961, added modern touches and altered the interior: the Williamses, notably, installed one of the area's first television sets and a candy-striped soda fountain soon after they moved in. The former French colony, in addition to installing twin swimming pools outside, has given the interior touches of the Ivory Coast through displays of various artifacts.

George and Lily Livingston had this mahogany staircase built into Livingston's Vale. It included a built-in organ and leads to a tiled veranda that had been pried from a Bavarian castle.

THE WINTER OF 1976–77 WAS A FRIGID, SNOWY ONE
in Washington, literally putting on ice the construction of the new
Japanese ambassador's residence, across the street from the National
Presbyterian Church and NBC's television facilities. Plans for a grand
opening on the April 29 national day had to be scrapped, and the celebration was held at the old neo-Georgian residence on Massachusetts
Avenue. Japanese cherry trees had been planted in readiness at the new
Nebraska Avenue location, a gleaming fountain and distinctive teahouse
were in place, but, Ambassador Fumihiko Togo lamented, "mostly, the
grounds are a sea of mud."

In 1972 the Japanese had purchased for $2 million the nearly
eight-acre site bordering the Swedish embassy grounds from "Sittie"
Parker, divorced wife of the board chairman of the Woodward &
Lothrop department store. In the late 1800s the property had been the
grounds for the prestigious Dumblane fox-hunting club on the Grass-
land estate of New Yorker S. S. Howland. The land was later part of
the sprawling Glover estate owned by Riggs National Bank president
and chairman Charles C. Glover. In addition to establishing Rock
Creek, Potomac, and the National Zoological parks, Glover had also
made possible the erection of American University buildings on his uptown land.

The Japanese razed the Parker house to make room for their
new building, designed by American-born architect Masao Kinoshita
of Watertown, Massachusetts. So hush-hush were negotiations, which
had begun as early as 1970, that not even the U.S. Office of Protocol
knew about them. The embassy staff had outgrown the old building,
had been leasing extra office space at the Watergate apartment building, and needed the ambassador's Massachusetts Avenue quarters for
chancery functions. One estimate placed construction costs of the new
residence and its furnishings at $12 million.

The Parker place had boasted what *Star-News* writer Betty Beale
called "fabulous trees," many 50 years old or more. "There are huge
dogwood trees, a tremendous old Russian mulberry tree, an osage orange tree and any number of large old oaks," Beale wrote in 1972. "The
big fruit of the osage orange is inedible but its very hard flexible wood
once made it excellent bow material for the Indians. 'It's still considered
the finest bow a sportsman can buy,' said Mrs. Parker."

Sittie Parker moved to a smaller house on Van Ness Street,
where, Beale reported, "she will be able to watch the growth of whatever the Japanese create." Dozens of trees were indeed felled, but the
Japanese imported others to replace them. As for the new house, an
embassy official told the *Washington Post* that it would have the "feel and
look" of a Japanese house. "In Japan, the traditional house is of wood
and paper. That would not be practical in the Washington climate. So
our new residence will be of stone and concrete." Its grand salon, longer
than the White House ballroom and reminiscent, one observer said, of
a huge hotel lobby, was designed to accommodate 500 for cocktails, its
drawing room comfortable for 40 dinner guests.

Entertainment at Ambassador and Madame Togo's housewarm-

RESIDENCE OF THE
AMBASSADOR OF JAPAN
4000 Nebraska Avenue, Northwest
Masao Kinoshita, Architect
═══ *1977* ═══

The Japanese ambas-
sador's residence
contains spaces that
are ultra-functional
and others that are
quietly contemplative.
Eight landscape artists
constructed the
gardens and pond.

ing, when it was finally ready in November 1977, included a fashion show by couture designer Hanae Mori of New York, Tokyo, and Paris. Madame Togo herself wore a Mori creation that the designer said had taken 40 days to create. Supreme Court Justice Potter Stewart, who was in attendance, described one of the gowns as "straight from the 1920s—the flapper age, you know." Guests were somewhat startled at the size of the house at a time of increasing energy consciousness; two stories rise above ground, two more dip below. "When you're an embassy, you don't concern yourself with such mundane things," the *Post* quoted one visitor. Visitors admired the house's hand-blocked wallpaper and shoji screens.

A "must-see" at the old Massachusetts Avenue address had been the ambassador's garden and *ippakutei,* or teahouse, which had been prebuilt in Japan and reassembled here. It continued in use for a time after the Nebraska Avenue facility was in place because the new structure had not been properly consecrated by a tea master. The garden of the new residence, according to the *Post,* even included a pond ("man-made but with real carp") and a waterfall (which once flooded the teahouse). An embassy publication notes that "in style and in conception [it] resembles the early nineteenth century garden of the Kogetsu-tei of Sugata-an in Matsue, designed by the great feudal lord and tea master, Fumai Matsudaira." The garden's centerpiece is another teahouse, also imported from Tokyo, overlooking a pond, "purposely designed to be large, to give the illusion of the tea house floating upon it." A guide for visitors explains the elaborate tea ceremony:

The tea ceremony house was dedicated in 1960 to 100 years of Japanese-U.S. relations. Behind a partly concealed panel, the host makes ceremonial preparations as guests enjoy the serene view.

The custom of drinking powdered tea in a tea ceremony was brought from China to Japan by a Buddhist monk, Eisai, toward the end of the 12th century. In the 16th century, the fundamentals of the tea ceremony were perfected by a Zen monk, Sen no Rikyu, who summarized its basic idea in four words: WA, KEI, SEI, and JAKU. WA is harmony, the harmony among people and with nature; KEI is respect, an expression of gratitude towards all things; SEI is purity; JAKU is tranquility of man and nature. Thus the spiritual foundation of Chanoya is derived from Zen Buddhism for which [the] essence of reality and beauty is simplicity.

While designed to evoke a contemplative Buddhist setting, the imperial-size residence, sprawling over 1.6 acres, has become the center of elaborate Kabuki plays, benefit balls, and displays of Japanese commerce and cultures—activities that now better represent a frenetic modern Japan.

AROUND A COUPLE OF BENDS BEHIND AMERICAN
University, on the edge of Spring Valley, sits one of Washington's most
contemporary diplomatic residences—and most faithful architecturally
to the nation whose ambassador it serves. Designed by South Korea's
fabled postwar Space Group architect, Swoo-Guen Kim—master architect of the 1988 Olympic Games complex in Seoul—and executed
by Washington architect Jack Samperton, it has all the solemn trappings of an upper-class Yi Dynasty villa. However, its 18,000-square-
foot floor space, ceremonial entrance, large reception hall, several
wings, and central courtyard would dwarf such residences in that nation. Kim died in 1986, before the building officially opened on October 3 of that year, Korea's Foundation Day holiday, Kae Chun Chal.
More than 1,000 people attended the housewarming without crowding
the residence. A few days earlier, Ambassador and Madame Kyung-
Won Kim had hosted members of the Spring Valley Citizens' Association, whose fears about having an embassy in their midst had been
soothed by the quiet dignity of both the building and its occupants.

The ideal Korean home faces south, has hills or mountains to its
north, a water source to the south, and is surrounded by trees. The
sunny southern exposure, murmuring stream, and shade from the summer sun are optimum, and Kim and Samperton delivered on all but the
hills, which are humble in Spring Valley.

The house sits on grounds once owned by Robert Whittier Dudley, the Washington lawyer and executive who, with his wife, Argentina,
daughter of a former ambassador from the Dominican Republic, raised
six children and entertained spectacularly at Gatesley, their Tudor-style
home built by the ubiquitous W. C. and A. N. Miller Company, devel-
opers of Spring Valley. In 1978, in turn, Dudley—despairing, neighbors
say, of D.C. taxes and intrusions onto the property by inebriated American University students—sold the house and its land to the Koreans
and moved to Maryland. The Space Group kept the house vacant for
many years and finally demolished it.

While the $4 million ambassadorial dwelling has many of the el-
ements of a fragile Korean structure, with wood and stucco predomi-
nating, the architects hid the supporting steel beams and opted for copper roofing rather than traditional clay roof tiles. Samperton said Kim
chose copper for the roofing because the green patina that would appear as it aged would blend with the natural surroundings. Wooden
columns, beams, staircases, and buttresses proliferate, as do pagodas,
lanterns, and a pond reminiscent of home. Wisconsin pine lamination,
which came in thousands of pieces that had to be meticulously pieced
together as one might master a sophisticated Lincoln Log set, masks the
steel skeleton. The courtyard's small pond is square with a round island
in its midst, a configuration derived from the Oriental philosophy of the
balance of life—Yin (the square-shaped pond as earth) and Yang (the
round island as the sky). Simplicity is served in the paper-covered
changhoji doors in the grand passageway to the second-story grand
banquet room. More than 300 of the panels for windows and doors
were constructed in Korea and installed by Korean craftworkers. Tra-

RESIDENCE OF THE
AMBASSADOR OF KOREA
4801 Glenbrook Road, Northwest
Swoo-Guen Kim, Architect
1986

The Korean ambas-
sador's residence
incorporates both
delicate ricepaper doors
and screens and
interlocking wood
lamination, stabilized
by artfully concealed
steel beams and a
copper roof.

ditional Korean ricepaper screens were used in windows, creating translucent screens using up to 10 layers of the paper. Also from Korea are rugs, musical instruments, lanterns, sculptures, and paintings.

Only one cherished Korean tradition seems lacking, but of necessity, given the building's function: privacy. *Washington Post* critic Benjamin Forgey, in his review of the house in 1986, noted, "The flaw has become ever more apparent as the splendid deciduous trees in the front yard have shed their leaves." That aside, though, Forgey observed, guests were charmed by the residence's white panels and lanterns, which delivered "a sense of being in another place and time. It was for such moments especially that this house was designed."

CHANCERY AND RESIDENCE OF THE AMBASSADOR OF LITHUANIA

A Henderson House

2622 16th Street, Northwest

George Oakley Totten, Jr., Architect

━━━━━ *1908* ━━━━━

━━━━━━ ━ ━━━━━━

Delicate table settings, figurines, and native dolls fill the old Lithuanian legation. Many had gathered dust in cold, closed-off rooms during the austere times before the nation's liberation.

FOR 50 YEARS UNTIL THE CYCLONIC EVENTS OF 1990 and 1991, the largest piece of free Lithuania was a 17,000-square-foot plot of land on 16th Street in Washington, an ocean away from the tormented Baltic homeland. On the property sat the valiant "symbolic embassy," the Lithuanian legation, presided over by a persevering chargé d'affaires and the two or three staff members whose salaries were paid by Lithuanian-American supporters and the old republic's U.S. gold reserves. These reserves had been frozen by the United States and pooled with those of the other subjugated Baltic states, Latvia and Estonia, by the Federal Reserve after the Soviet army marched into tiny, 959-square-mile Lithuania in June 1940 and installed a "People's Government" parliament at the point of a gun. Under first the Bolsheviks, then Hitler as his forces drove toward Leningrad, then the "liberating" Soviets again, hundreds of thousands of Lithuanians were shipped to gulags, and almost all of the nation's Jews were massacred.

Lithuania had been a proud medieval kingdom. The Vytis, a sword-wielding knight on a charger, carrying a shield with the double-cross (‡), believed to symbolize the union of a Lithuanian prince and his Polish bride, is still the national emblem, and the Lithuanian language is one of the oldest living tongues. But Lithuania has also endured the indignities of many intrusions, first by Russia's Peter the Great and later by Germany's Kaiser Wilhelm, and, worst of all, following 22 years of fragile independence after the Treaty of Versailles, by the Red Army on the heels of the duplicitous 1939 Molotov-Ribbentrop Pact.

The Lithuanian minister to Washington at the time, Povilas Zadeikis, refused the demand that he turn over his legation to Soviet control, and he held forth there for another 18 years. The Italianate house with its tower had been one of a dozen or so built for U.S. Senator and Mrs. John B. Henderson, who had attempted to create a regal 16th Street diplomatic neighborhood just after the turn of the century (see page 90). In the first 15 years following its completion in 1908, this mansion was rented off and on to individual envoys, but it frequently stood empty. Marc Peter, the Swiss minister to the United States, had occupied the house just before Mary Foote Henderson sold it to the government of Lithuania for $90,000 in 1924. She received $5,000 down and then refused to accept additional payments, despite many efforts by the Lithuanians to proffer them. Following her death in 1931, the estate and the Lithuanian government settled the balance.

Nine years later, when Lithuania was overrun by Red Army troops, the United States, with a handful of other nations, while gingerly avoiding full diplomatic recognition of legitimate Lithuania, refused to acknowledge the little nation's absorption into the Soviet Union. In the years that followed, Zadeikis was forced to work in heavy-hearted limbo. He and his successors had no nation to which to report and no way to visit or even correspond with their compatriots. Funds to keep up the aging house, with its leaking roof and weed-choked garden, including rue, a herb that figures in national folklore, were meager.

Still, once a year, on February 16, the legation would sponsor a

modest cocktail reception, attended mainly by Lithuanian Americans and a few members of diplomatic society, to mark the 1918 independence anniversary. Ironically, two of the guests who did show up at the legation's 20th-anniversary independence party in 1938 were Ambassador and Madame Alexander Troyanovsky of the Soviet embassy, who, a society correspondent reported, hobnobbed with the hosts and guests from Latvia and Estonia. This conviviality reigned a year before Joseph Stalin's connivance with Adolf Hitler would consign all three nations to Soviet domination.

The *Washington Star* described Chargé d'Affaires Stasys A. Backis, then 72, as a "sad-eyed man without a country." On this occasion, Backis turned to a map of his homeland, hanging in the darkened hallway outside his office, and pointed to Joniskelis, the town of his birth on the River Musa. "He has not been there for 40 years," wrote *Star* reporter John Sherwood, "and will never be able to return."

Somehow the mission held on. Stasys Lozoraitis, Jr., who arrived as chargé in Washington in 1987 after a 17-year stint as chief of the Lithuanian mission to the Vatican, recalls, "It was like crossing the desert, having to concentrate on survival, of where we had to go, and of having the determination to get there. We had this. We would never give up, never give up, even after receiving blow after blow. We were waiting for history to turn, since history is so full of surprises. Of course it did, but, candidly, we thought we were working for the next generation, or if not some point 20 years from now, maybe 50 years, maybe 100 years."

The mansion, which Lithuanian Americans paid to have minimally renovated in the 1980s, served as a symbol over the years, "a silent, beautiful lady," Lozoraitis says. Meanwhile Lozoraitis and his wife began to dress up the 31-room mansion, restoring a second-floor reception area with brocaded walls and Renaissance Revival details to its former glory and installing contemporary and folk art pieces. In the basement was found a 1939 canvas by painter Petras Kalpokas commemorating the signing of the Lithuanian declaration of independence in 1918, now placed prominently in the embassy's entrance hall.

Then, in 1990, what had been the improbable dream for "The Land of Northern Gold" (coined for the amber yielded from the Baltic Sea) happened with breathtaking speed. Lithuania, whose independence movement, Sajudis, had been above-board as early as 1988, was the first Baltic nation to declare its separation from the U.S.S.R., for which it suffered both Moscow's economic boycott and deadly provocations involving Soviet troops. Following the foiled Moscow coup of August 1991, Soviet President Mikhail Gorbachev announced that he was prepared to release the Balts from Soviet control. "What has happened to my country is one of history's miracles," Minister Lozoraitis said as he prepared to leave on a trip to the Holy See, where he was concurrently the Lithuanian representative. He left knowing that he would be bringing back credentials to President Bush that would change his rank to ambassador and the suddenly sunny legation into a full embassy.

It took some time for Mary Foote Henderson, denizen of 16th Street's Embassy Row, to get the Lithuanians to buy the Italianate house that bore some of the same brooding features of her own "castle."

FAMILIAR NAMES POP UP IN THE HISTORY OF THE
Grand Duchy of Luxembourg's Louis XV limestone and brick manor
on Massachusetts Avenue. The Kalorama Heights land on which it sits
was owned by Katherine Medill McCormick (see page 27). The property passed through one more owner before Alexander and Margaret
Gray Stewart bought it in 1908 and commissioned the prominent New
York architects Jules Henri de Sibour and Bruce Price to build a house.
De Sibour, a native of France and trained in Paris, was active in Washington, where he built the Chevy Chase Club, Howard University's Science Hall, and many residences, including two separate Kalorama Road
homes for W. W. Lawrence that became the residences of the ambassadors of France and Portugal. The construction cost of the Stewarts'
new four-story home was estimated at $92,000.

Alexander Stewart had been a congressman from Wisconsin
who made his fortune buying huge chunks of prime Midwest timber-
land. The sons of Scottish immigrants to New Brunswick, he and his
brother John immigrated to the United States and made their way to
bustling Milwaukee in the 1850s. From there, so the story goes, he
walked to Wausau, 170 miles as the crow flies, in the Wisconsin timber
country. The young men took jobs as millhands at $16 a month but
asked to be paid in lumber and shingles, which they saved and then
floated down the Mississippi River to St. Louis and sold at a handsome
price. The Stewarts soon managed, then owned, Wausau's largest lumber mill. Alexander ventured into politics, served three terms in the
House of Representatives, and stayed in Washington after leaving
Congress in 1900. After Stewart's death in 1912 from a fall while visiting a paper mill, his wife and three daughters, Helen, Margaret, and
Mary (and Helen and Margaret's husbands), in various turns, lived in
the house until 1937, when, according to a report of the U.S. Commission of Fine Arts, Mary left it vacant until she sold it in 1941 to H.R.H.
Charlotte, the grand duchess of Luxembourg, for $40,000, far less than
the $104,000 assessed value of the property. "The house is a handsome
one and would have been, later, an excellent site for an uptown hotel,"
society columnist Helen Essary commented. "The coat-of-arms of the
little principality is being cut in stone above the door."

The grand duchess did not live in the house, the commission report continues, "but spent her time in Montreal and London, where her
ministers in exile were located during the German occupation of her
country." Instead, the duchy, which had maintained a legation at the
Shoreham Hotel, moved those functions to the Massachusetts Avenue
house. The grand duchess's mother, Dowager Grand Duchess Maria
Anna, did live in the house. When Maria Anna moved to town in 1941,
the *Washington Times-Herald* noted, "Washington, which has grown a little blasé over visiting royalty, can sit up and take notice. . . . Because of
her advanced age—80 years—and because she is mourning for the
death of a member of her family, there will be no entertaining, either
formal or otherwise." The dowager grand duchess died a year later. In
September 1944 the Luxembourg legation was the first, and only, diplomatic establishment to celebrate openly the Allies' liberation of Axis-

RESIDENCE OF THE
AMBASSADOR
OF LUXEMBOURG
Stewart House
2200 Massachusetts Avenue, Northwest
J. Henri de Sibour and Bruce Price, Architects
1908

69

operated countries in Europe. Minister Hughes Le Gallais raised the red, white, and blue flag of his nation atop the balcony of the legation.

Luxembourg's legation received embassy status in 1955, and seven years later its government bought a rowhouse building in the block, at 2210 Massachusetts—formerly the Israeli chancery—for use as a chancery, then purchased the main house for $160,000 from the grand duchess and made it the ambassador's residence.

Washington Post columnist Dorothy McCardle dropped by and was overcome by "the sudden feeling that you have been transported into the ancestral home of the descendants of Marco Polo. All around you are reminders of Venice, hometown of the famous explorer and also of Madame Le Gallais. . . . You are surrounded by priceless scrolls, paintings, vases, sculpture and chests from the Orient, lands first opened up to Western eyes by Italy's most famous traveling man back in the thirteenth century."

Behind an entrance hall statue in the Luxembourg ambassador's home, the stairway's carved balustrade depicts various flora and fauna. Opposite: Representative Alexander Stewart lived in this mansion only four years before his accidental death.

MEXICAN CULTURAL INSTITUTE

MacVeagh House

2829 16th Street, Northwest

Nathan Wyeth, Architect

1911

The music room of the Mexican Cultural Institute features an organ and a chair in the Louis XIII style. Following pages: The sweeping hallway mural is a fresco by Roberto Cueva del Rio.

WASHINGTON SOCIETY WAS AGOG IN 1911 AS GEORGE A. Fuller Company laborers put the finishing touches on an imposing four-story, buff-brick mansion on 16th Street in what was becoming the city's newest enclave of fashionable residences and embassies. Part of the land had been purchased from Mary Foote Henderson, the redoubtable developer of Meridian Hill, by a trust appointed by the mansion's secret owner. Repeated inquiries to workmen and the building's designer, Nathan Wyeth of New York — who had recently completed a house for Hattie Sanger Pullman down the street (later to be the Imperial Russian embassy) — elicited no information on the owner of this magnificent new structure, and the gossip intensified.

Among several persons who wangled private tours was William Howard Taft's secretary of the treasury, Franklin MacVeagh. MacVeagh and his wife, Emily, lived in another famous Washington house, Marshall Field's former Pink Palace, a stone's throw away. The secretary, who had been schooled in law but made his fortune as a wholesale grocer in Chicago, also dabbled in architecture. On Christmas eve, according to legend, as the MacVeaghs strolled through the new house, completely furnished and tidy, MacVeagh complimented the "exquisite taste" of the mystery owner. "Well if you like it," Emily MacVeagh was said to have replied, "you may have it as a Christmas gift!" As the story goes, Emily MacVeagh had been the mystery owner all along.

Indeed, a Merry Christmas present was the $120,000 home, with its lavish music room emulating the one in the French royal palace at Fontainebleau, pipe organ and chimes, the largest dining room in the city, and 14-carat gold leaf on the walls of the drawing room. A 1925 *Washington Star* article described the worth of this gilt wallpaper as "almost equal to what an average man might produce in a lifetime." (A bubble-burster, columnist Evelyn Peyton Gordon, writing in the *Washington Daily News* after touring the mansion, would flatly declare 21 years later, "I want to add that the renowned gold-leaf on the drawing room walls was not removed by the Ambassador and sent to Mexico. Actually there was no gold-leaf. It was only paint — and very dirty.")

When the MacVeaghs moved in and toasted their new home, President Taft and his debutante daughter, Helen, were the guests of honor. So taxing was the electrical overload of the affair that the lights went out, and Mary Foote Henderson and others scurried to their homes to find candles.

After a long illness, Emily MacVeagh died in 1916. Her husband moved out of the 26-room house and returned to Chicago, saying he could not bear to live in a place that so reminded him of his beloved Emily. He leased it to Assistant Secretary of State Breckinridge Long, who put the home at the disposal of Lord Balfour, head of the British mission, and then King Albert and Queen Elizabeth of Belgium during their visit in 1919. In 1921 MacVeagh sold the residence and many of its furnishings to the government of Mexico for $330,000. He asked two concessions of the Mexicans — that they make no significant alterations during his lifetime, and that his favorite servant be given lifetime employment.

The MacVeaghs
entertained the capital's
glitterati in the music
room of the house
that had been
Emily MacVeagh's
surprise Christmas
gift to her husband.
When she died,
Franklin moved out.

Both were granted, if one does not count a chancery wing, garage, and portico entrance, which the Mexicans immediately added. They also filled the house with Mexican art, including Aztec sculpture. After MacVeagh's death, at age 97 in 1934, Ambassador Manuel Tellez—later dean of the city's diplomatic corps—continued the "Mexicanization" of the home, dispersing some of the MacVeagh furnishings and turning parts of the house into a model Mexican salon. Native flowers, cacti, and other plants were added to the roof garden; colorful Mayan murals were painted; and strolling guitarists became a fixture at receptions. A second-floor mural, part of a series by Cuevo Del Rio that rise along a grand staircase from the first floor to the third, depicts the solidarity of Western Hemisphere nations. The gold, or gold-colored, wallcovering disappeared. In 1941 the embassy covered the walls of the solarium with Talavera tiles from the city of Puebla, which depict two great Mexican volcanoes as well as the coats of arms of the nation and its 29 states, and also added a fountain.

After another renovation in 1946, much Mexican silver was brought into the house, including tableware and small decorative objects, and the "Mexicanization" was complete.

One of the most memorable affairs in the building, in 1957, feted the celebrated Mexican comedian Cantinflas. After the ambassador moved out in the late 1980s, the house became the Mexican Cultural Institute, which offers a wide range of programs and art exhibitions throughout the year.

76

"'THE GLORY THAT WAS GREECE, AND THE GRAN-
deur that was Rome' were nothing," reported the *Washington Post* in
1933, "compared to the magnificence that was Russia when a Russian
Ambassador held forth in regal splendor in the days of the Tsar." The
ambassador's post, three blocks from the White House, was a five-
story, stone and beige-brick house built by New York architect Nathan
Wyeth for Hattie Sanger Pullman, widow of the Chicago sleeping-car
magnate. (Wyeth's other Washington credits are the Key Bridge,
Columbia Hospital for Women, and the White House's Oval Office.)
Many years later, the Beaux Arts structure would get a tepid review
from the U.S. Commission of Fine Arts: "The Pullman residence as designed by Wyeth is an attempt at originality, if only because it is not
historically 'correct.' Neither is it exceptional for its time, unless size
and costliness of materials are criteria for excellence."

Hattie Pullman, an energetic businesswoman and philanthropist, "is said to have blown three million dollars in an abortive attempt
to crash society here in the Wilson era," according to Robert Smith and
Eric Sevareid in *Washington: Magnificent Capital*. She intended the house
for her daughter and son-in-law, Congressman Frank O. Lowden, but
neither Mrs. Pullman nor the Lowdens ever lived at 1125 16th Street.
Neither did its next owner, Natalie Harris Hammond, who, with her
husband, John Hays Hammond, had a perfectly comfortable mansion
(now the French ambassador's residence) on Kalorama Road. Within
six months in 1913, she sold the 16th Street building for $350,000 to the
government of imperial Russia, which immediately also bought the lot
next door on which to build a chancery.

Over from the old czarist embassy on Rhode Island Avenue
strode Ambassador George Bakhmeteff, who had married an American, Marie Beale, a Washington millionaire and daughter of the owner
of Decatur House (see page 13). Marie Bakhmeteff put her staff of 40
(not counting the chef and kitchen help) to work taking care of the 64-
room house. Came the Russian Revolution in 1917, the Bakhmeteffs re-
paired to their house in Paris, followed by a shipment of the Pullman
house's best antiques, spared from the Bolshevik onslaught. For a time
the provisional government led by Alexander Kerensky, which itself
was busy dodging the Bolsheviks, maintained the house with Bakhmeteff still theoretically on the job. Having little else to do, the caretaker
staff was spotted amazing Washingtonians with their skating prowess
on nearby ponds and neighborhood rinks.

The U.S. government broke diplomatic relations with the Soviets in 1922, the caretakers disappeared, and the embassy sat empty, its
furnishings gathering dust, for 12 years. Once during that time, someone strung a huge banner across the entranceway reading, "Rasputin
closed this embassy. But he opens at Loew's Columbia — 'Rasputin and
the Empress.'" In 1933 a moving van pulled up, and workers removed
boxes of papers from the days of the imperial regime. After the Roosevelt administration recognized the Stalinist government a year later, the
building was reopened by new Communist occupants.

Stalin's ambassador, Alexander Troyanovsky, unshuttered the

CHANCERY AND RESIDENCE
OF THE AMBASSADOR
OF THE RUSSIAN REPUBLIC
Pullman House
1125 16th Street, Northwest
Nathan Wyeth, Architect
— 1910 —

The Soviets turned
Hattie Pullman's
Edwardian ballroom,
with its elaborate
columns and cande-
labra — now electri-
fied — into a reception
room, but the tradition
of utterly bourgeois
festivities lived on.

Pullman house for a gala opening party, where the flag of the hammer and sickle was unfurled and Mrs. Woodrow Wilson, Secretary of State and Mrs. Cordell Hull, and lawyer Clarence Darrow were among the glitterati. Secretary of Labor Frances Perkins, another guest, celebrated her birthday in the midst of four floors of buffet lines. So envious were the uninvited that several donned formal attire and tried to crash the party, but, according to Hope Ridings Miller, "a platoon of door checkers barred the uninvited proletariat, and the rebuffed contingent had to take an embarrassed exit through a throng of curious spectators jamming 16th Street."

The guests could not help but notice a huge portrait of Comrade Stalin hanging incongruously in the vortex of capitalist excess, the Versailles-inspired ballroom. By 1959, when Premier Nikita Khrushchev paid a visit and threw a party of his own for the Eisenhowers and a few hundred friends, Stalin's portrait was nowhere to be found. For the Khrushchev affair, the Soviets borrowed the Mayflower Hotel's fabled gold service, flew in the chef and most of the food from Moscow, and topped off the evening with servings of Baked Alaska (an attempt at a lighthearted bow to the former Russian outpost), each topped with a red (what else?) twinkling, battery-powered light.

The Pullman house had been refurbished by New York architect Eugene Schoen when the Communists first moved in. He was instructed to decorate it in an Art Moderne style but declined, saying it would be sinful to tear out gilded and rococo furnishings that would cost $2.5 million (in 1933 dollars) to replace. Vowing he would not touch "the last hair of the last cupid," Schoen stuck to pedestrian improvements like a central vacuum-cleaning system and new kitchens and baths.

By Cold War days of the 1950s through the 1970s, two other characteristics of the building stood out: its array of 12 antennae on the mansard roof (the Soviets were doing more than watching Walter Cronkite), and the closed and heavily draped windows. As the thermostat seemed to be perpetually set at 80 degrees, whatever the weather, one visitor called the embassy "the most overheated building since those destroyed in the Chicago fire." At an embassy party marking the publication of a cookbook on Russian cuisine, writer Cleveland Amory, remarking on the abundance of non-Slavic chowhounds and paucity of Soviet hosts, cracked, "They're all upstairs taking showers because the air is so bad in here."

There were a few, but only a few, other parties for outsiders hosted by the suspicious Soviets in their gold-braided uniforms. One, in honor

---

When the Soviets and Americans finally established diplomatic relations after a 12-year hiatus, Stalin quickly sent over his new ambassador to the United States. The *Washington Daily News*'s Evelyn Peyton Gordon described Washington's reaction: "When Ambassador Alexander Antonovich Troyanovsky set foot here, Washingtonians were surprised that he didn't wear a long beard and carry a knife in his teeth," she wrote. "Such were our ideas of the new regime of Russia." Americans had formed some of their notions of Russianness from the imperial minister to Washington in President John Tyler's day, 90 years earlier. Baron de Bodisco was a bachelor in his late 50s and a regular at Henry Clay's poker games. One night he arose from the game, down $1,000. "Ladees and gentlemans," the *Washington Times-Herald* quotes him as having said, "it is very disagree duty to make it announce that these receptions must have an end and to declare them at an end for the present because why? The fund for them ladees and gentlemans is exhaust." The baron recovered sufficient funds to wed the 16-year-old daughter of the U.S. adjutant general. The *Times-Herald* story described the radiant bride, the groom in "dyed whiskers and hair," the groomsmen, all over 50 and some "tottering on the verge of septuagenarianism," and the bridesmaids, all aged 14 to 16.

of the Apollo-Soyuz space flight in 1975 and attended by the cosmonauts and astronauts, featured a four-foot-high cheese rocket. The most extravagant bash of all occurred each October, ironically celebrating the revolution of the proletariat. One party was described by *Collier's* writer Andrew Tully as laying out "enough fancy food and liquor to nourish and intoxicate a Russian village for a month."

When Soviet Ambassador Georgi Nikolayevich Zaroubin presented his credentials to President Harry Truman in 1952, he announced that he would like to promote peace and take in a Washington Senators' baseball game. "Georgi Zaroubin can be as charming as he likes, but he's not kidding anybody," Tully wrote. "The people who deal with him know his background, and after he shakes their hand they always check to see how many fingers they've got left." That background included tours of duty in Canada when a spy ring was exposed and in Great Britain when Klaus Fuchs confessed to passing atomic-energy secrets to the Kremlin.

The 500-member Soviet diplomatic staff, the largest in Washington, lived painfully circumscribed lives. The staff was forbidden to mix with the population; all but the ambassador required approval to see a movie or accept a dinner invitation. Except on Revolution Day, the only sanctioned embassy parties involved diplomats from the Eastern Bloc nations, where, Tully reported, the Russians looked down on their colleagues, "and the satellites in turn defer to the Russians and, often, hate their guts." Entertainment—typically somber music and turgid films—was a study in drabness. Only the top embassy staff was permitted time off for a visit to Rehoboth Beach, Delaware, site of a summer diplomatic colony, where, presumably, KGB minions in bathing suits kept a close eye on them. Several Soviet diplomatic families lived in connecting communal houses on 21st Street; their youngsters, eight and under, studied Russian and French but were forbidden to learn English; older children were shipped back to the Soviet Union for a proper education. Whenever touch-up work was needed inside the old Pullman house, guards watched the workers' every move. One sentry was reported to have told a painter, "Please, comrade, don't blame us. We don't even trust ourselves."

Security precautions were prudent, as protesters regularly demonstrated outside. In 1968 a bomb, tossed before dawn, took a chunk out of the building's stone sills and iron grillwork.

Beginning in 1962, both the Soviet and U.S. governments laid plans for new facilities in each other's capitals. After two unsuccessful at-

A portrait of V. I. Lenin outlasted, at least for a time, the "Second Russian Revolution" that ousted the Communist leadership in 1991 as envoys struggled with an uncertain national identity.

tempts to locate a new embassy compound in residential areas of the District of Columbia, the Soviets did succeed in finding space, including the Nathaniel Luttrell mansion at Connecticut Avenue and Columbia Road. Finally an almost brick-for-brick reciprocal deal was cut in 1969 to build a new U.S. embassy in Moscow (what became the famous "bug"-infested structure built but never occupied) and a sprawling Soviet government complex on Mount Alto, the highest point in the city. The land, offered rent-free for 85 years, is on the 12.5-acre site of a former veterans' hospital not far from the Washington National Cathedral. Workers were closely supervised; technicians from Moscow installed every electronic component (including an even more impressive array of antennae). The embassy ordered the windows fabricated on site rather than at a factory. American and Soviet workers on the project shared their lunch hours in nearby Wisconsin Avenue taverns, where vodka outsold beer three to one.

At first it seemed that the Soviets would unload the Pullman house as a decadent reminder of their nation's czarist past. Senator Joseph Montoya of New Mexico, whose profession was real estate, tried to buy the building, but Ambassador Anatoly Dobrynin declined, saying his government would keep the 16th Street address "as a recreation center for our staff." Indeed the Soviets kept it, for the State Department forbade their moving the chancery or the ambassador's residence to Mount Alto until its own second try at building an eavesdropping-proof embassy in Moscow was complete.

The dorms and peripheral facilities at the new embassy were in use, however, during Mikhail Gorbachev's historic period of *glasnost* and *perestroika,* as well as the astounding "Second Russian Revolution"—the failed Moscow coup of 1991 that accelerated the dissolution of the Communist empire. It was during this period that we took our photographs for *Embassies of Washington.* A huge portrait of Vladimir Lenin, hanging at the top of the sweeping grand staircase, was still much in evidence, and an embassy official explained that, whether or not Communism was in its death throes, hundreds of thousands of Soviet citizens had given their lives in Lenin's name at the walls of Leningrad. Since then, the Soviet embassy has become the Embassy of the Russian Republic, with office space offered to other republics until further arrangements can be made. Left unclear was the prognosis for a curtain over the proscenium arch at the new embassy's 400-seat theater, on which had been stitched a slogan: "Forward the Victory of Communism."

Two other vestiges of a discredited era marked the old Pullman House: the Soviet hammer-and-sickle flag and an array of antennae once employed for far more than improving television reception.

THE EMBASSIES OF WASHINGTON ARE KNOWN FOR their monumental architecture, their colorful human legacies, their lavish social encounters, and their intrigue. But one diplomatic building, housing the ambassador of the Republic of South Africa, is renowned for a single room. The building, erected in 1936 to house the South African legation before it achieved embassy status, features a dining room paneled in rare native "stinkhout," or stinkwood. The now-rare, rock-hard, walnut-like wood, which shows up in expensive desks and bookcases throughout the house, takes two centuries to mature, so it is vigorously protected. The name of the *Ocotea bullata* tree comes from the rancid odor of the wood when it is first cut.

The residence was designed by architect John J. Whelan, who, five years earlier, had supervised erection of the Norwegian legation farther up Massachusetts Avenue. According to an embassy publication, Minister Ralph Close admonished Whelan to be sure "the exterior should, without being in any way ornate, at least be chaste and dignified and such as South Africans can reasonably be proud of." The intent was to feature the 18th-century Cape Dutch architecture of the Cape of Good Hope, but Indiana limestone was substituted for the traditional whitewashed plaster. The building's portico is a replica of the Kat balcony in the pentagonal castle in Cape Town, built by the Dutch East India Company in the 17th century.

Architect Whelan designed not only the building but also the residence's dining-room tables and chairs. Old Cape Dutch cabinets, breakfronts, trousseau "kists," or chests, and paintings by South African artists have been added by ambassadors over the years. Among these are depictions of a Transvaal landscape, a Cape Town fishing scene, and a series of Zulu portraits. A chancery annex, completed in 1965, is reached through the second-floor library. It is a replica of an 18th-century Dutch homestead.

Not surprisingly, considering the international tumult sparked by South Africa's apartheid policies, the embassy compound has been a frequent target of protests. Free South Africa movement leaders and celebrities, including, in 1975, singer Stevie Wonder, have periodically been arrested for demonstrating within 500 feet of an embassy. "What happens when an embassy becomes beleaguered?" asked the *Washington Star*'s Joy Billington in 1978. "Do important people still go to that ambassador's parties, or do they tend to avoid them? The answer appears to be that most Washingtonians don't care about politics, providing the 'lamb chop' is well cooked and the wines good."

The "lamb chop" reference was to the "Lamb Chop Principle," articulated, according to Billington, by either the late famous Washington hostess Perle Mesta or the noted journalist Joseph Alsop, that a good meal and pleasant company will always draw a crowd. Without doubt, South African ambassadors have had a more taxing challenge than most to explain their country's policies. As apartheid laws are dismantled by the Pretoria government, the task of representing the nation in Washington figures to get smoother.

RESIDENCE OF
THE AMBASSADOR OF
SOUTH AFRICA
3101 Massachusetts Avenue, Northwest
John J. Whelan, Architect
1936

Following pages:
Stinkwood, from which
the South African
ambassador's dining-
room paneling, chairs,
table, and buffet
are carved, is now a
carefully protected flora.
Ceramic and clay
figures, clay pots, and
ostrich-egg beads dot
the residence.

RESIDENCE OF THE
AMBASSADOR OF SPAIN

A Henderson House

2801 16th Street, Northwest

George Oakley Totten, Architect

1923

*The Spanish ambas-
sador's patio is an
imitation of a typical
Andalusian courtyard,
with its window
ironwork, tiled floor,
fountain, and
tiled portrait of
the Blessed Virgin.*

THE STORY OF THIS ELEGANT AMBASSADORIAL residence is enmeshed in a tale of *Gone with the Wind* proportions, complete with its own Tara and headstrong female lead.

Inside Boundary Castle, the turreted brownstone fortress that dominated the west side of the 2200 block of 16th Street at the turn of the century, the woman whom the *Washington Star* called "Washington's social arbiter," Mary Foote Henderson, hatched a grand plan: to build, on hundreds of surrounding acres, several other manor houses and rent them, or sell them at cost, to foreign governments as showplaces for their diplomatic corps, thus creating a glorious Embassy Hill on Meridian Heights (later, Hill) and cleaning up the seedy neighborhood. As early as 1890, Mary Henderson and her husband, John—the former U.S. senator from Missouri, friend of Abraham Lincoln, and author of the Thirteenth Amendment abolishing slavery—methodically began to purchase more than 300 parcels of land surrounding the castle, sweeping away shanties, meager vegetable plots, and unsightly billboards as they went. From his days in banking and real estate, the senator had amassed a fortune reputed to exceed $20 million. When he was voted out of office for siding with Andrew Johnson in the president's impeachment proceedings, Henderson told his wife, according to a story in *The American Weekly,* "We have nothing to worry about. My fortune is your fortune. We'll enjoy it."

The view from the castle on Boundary Street (now Florida Avenue) on the upper ridge of Washington civility, down to the White House and Washington Monument, had been anything but the most majestic in the low-lying capital, but after her husband's death in 1913, Mary Foote Henderson determined to make it so. Having once founded an art school in St. Louis, she retained an amateur's interest in architecture. After drawing her own preliminary sketches of the diplomats' homes, she dipped into the Henderson fortune and commissioned her favorite architect, George Oakley Totten, Jr., and others to build a dozen separate villas on the heights. "When a diplomat desires a new home in Washington, his thoughts turn towards Mrs. Henderson," wrote G. L. Waddell in the *National Republic* in 1927. "He holds a consultation with the brisk little mistress of Boundary Castle, and before long, there is another national crest displayed on Embassy Hill."

All the while, the widow Henderson carried the torch for her rehabilitated main street. Wrote James M. Goode in *Capital Losses,* "It was a familiar sight to see her with her gardener planting shrubbery along 16th Street." She convinced city commissioners to rename 16th Street "Avenue of the Presidents" but could savor the victory all too briefly. Annoyed at having to alter their stationery and house signs and to hunt for 16th Street between 15th and 17th, her neighbors quickly got "Avenue of the Presidents" changed back to its more prosaic designation.

Beginning with a new embassy for France, however, Mary Henderson's diplomatic colony sprouted nicely and soon included stately homes for the ministers of Ecuador, Spain, Mexico, Cuba, Poland, Lithuania, and the Netherlands. Most had been designed from the start

with the architecture of the host nation in mind. One that was not was the Spanish embassy, which, because of another Henderson brainstorm, was of "American" design. In 1922 Henderson formally offered to donate the palatial residence that Totten was building on the east side of the 2800 block of 16th Street to the federal government as a vice presidential château. No way, huffed Florence Harding, the nation's First Lady. There would not be any regal billeting for a mere vice president: "Do you think I'm going to have those Coolidges living in a home like *that*?" she exclaimed. Congress, too, did not believe that the vice president, then quietly ensconced at the Willard Hotel, could afford the lifestyle that went with such quarters, donated or otherwise, and declined the offer.

The Red Living Room was the ballroom in what was originally envisioned as a U.S. vice president's abode. The 18th-century painting over the fireplace is of Queen Isabel Farnesio, wife of Philip V.

The pipe dream of a vice presidential château, on top of Mary Henderson's earlier fancy, also rejected, that the presidential family itself ought to move to Meridian Hill, sounded an alarm with her granddaughter and only heir, Beatrice Henderson Wholean. It was not difficult to come up with proven eccentricities with which to tar the old dowager, for the headstrong Mary Henderson had drained the contents of Henderson Castle's renowned wine cellar into the 16th Street gutter in a show of support for Prohibition; railed against flesh-toned silk stockings and high-heeled shoes and required her maids to wear almost floor-length Victorian skirts well into the age of "flappers"; so disdained meat that she once served bananas shaped to look like pork chops; attacked the "poison vices" of "the drunkard, the glutton and the tobacco hog" in the best-known of her many books, the 700-page *The Aristocracy of Health;* ridden, twice a day, to the Lincoln Memorial, where she would walk twice around its reflecting pool; and, also twice, been hauled before a District of Columbia judge for cutting down trees that obstructed her view of the White House.

What, asked Beatrice Wholean, was to prevent this dervish, when she'd finished giving away buildings to official Washington, from frivolously dissipating all of her holdings? The granddaughter sought to have her institutionalized, only to lose her courtroom standing when Mary Henderson proved her to be an adoptee without the proper bloodlines for such a challenge. (After Henderson's death, at 90, at her summer home in Maine in 1931, the $6 million estate was left to her Japanese private secretary, Jesse S. Shima, who, after yet another court challenge that delighted society-page voyeurs, eventually divvied it up with granddaughter Beatrice.)

Mary Foote Henderson's vice presidential pretensions for 2801 16th Street having faded, she began touting the property as an ideal embassy for the government of Mexico, then seeking a location, but Mexico selected another estate altogether just up the street in the same block as 2801, and Totten's cavernous creation stood empty for three years. In 1926 the Spanish government—already a Henderson tenant at 2620 16th—decided to move its embassy to 2801. The Spaniards soon added to the main building a winter garden, fountain, hand-painted tiles from Seville and Valencia, wrought-iron doors and grilles from Toledo, and wainscoting. Construction also began on a new chancery (designed by a different architect, Jules Henri de Sibour), with an entrance facing in the other direction, on 15th Street. Particularly striking on the main building's patio-conservatory to this day is a mosaic of the Madonna de Los Reyes, patroness of Seville.

Although Hope Ridings Miller described the white stone Spanish embassy as having been inspired by "a Venetian palace," it is snootily dismissed, in *Homes of Interest In and Around Washington*, as "grand adobe style," with "badly scaled Beaux-Arts attachments" that work into a "California mission" look. The "frenzy of balustrades which in Totten's enthusiasm wrap about the facade and down the elliptical drive . . . do serve a happy purpose," the author states, in that they "draw attention away from details that, with height, decrease in quality."

The Spanish embassy has been redecorated several times since 1949. It had fallen into disrepair from 1936 to 1939, during the nation's civil war, a *Washington Daily News* reporter noting that the ballroom had been turned into a storeroom but was finally "taking shape as a beautiful drawing room." Paintings by Spanish masters, including Goya, and 17th-century Flemish tapestries continue to enhance the interior.

Further renovation in 1955 was supervised by Archduke Franz Josef of Spain and his wife, Princess Marta, who had established an interior-decorating shop in New York. "French is the diplomatic language, so I will make the ballroom a French room, all crystally and white and gold," the princess told the *Evening Star*. Ambassador José Maria Areilza also rehung the large portraits of King Alfonso XIII and Queen Victoria Eugenia that had been removed in 1931 with the end of the Spanish monarchy.

Other ambassadors and their wives have since made alterations to the patio-conservatory and have added flocked silk wall coverings in the drawing room and ballroom, where chandeliers from La Granja crystal works near Segovia, Spain, and Flemish tapestries also hang. Prominent during the tenure of several envoys have been artworks on loan from the Prado or brought from previous tours of duty in South America. "Badly scaled" or not, the Spanish embassy has been a featured station on the Washington diplomatic trail, and the Spaniards have liked it so well that they have stayed in one spot longer than any other foreign government.

As for Mary Foote Henderson's sandstone castle that started it all, it outlasted the feisty dowager by 18 years. When it was razed in 1949, only the entrance posts were left standing.

A silver urn is one of many Spanish touches added by ambassadors and their wives to what George Oakley Totten had originally designed as one of his few strictly "American" houses.

93

━━━━ ᴇ⊓⌐ᴏ ━━━━

RESIDENCE OF THE
AMBASSADOR OF SWEDEN

David Lawrence House

3900 Nebraska Avenue, Northwest

Arthur Heaton, Architect

━━ 1923 ━━

*Architect Arthur
Heaton was inspired by
Spanish architecture
when he designed
this house on
Nebraska Avenue.
The three crowns —
Sweden's national
symbol — are one of the
few exterior Swedish
embellishments.*

SIR WILLIAM GILBERT, OF GILBERT AND SULLIVAN, had a point when he wrote, "Things are seldom what they seem," and you can prove it at the Swedish ambassador's residence in Washington. The home, designed for *U.S. News & World Report* founder David Lawrence by architect Arthur Heaton in 1923, is a full-blown Spanish-style hacienda, complete with red-tiled roof, set on eight acres of impeccably landscaped grounds — hardly the place you'd expect to hail Sweden's Martin's Goose Day or sip mulled glögg on the feast of Saint Lucia. There are even Mexican tin plates and a large Spanish refectory table inside to complete the effect, and the cultural confusion continues with Flemish tapestries — bought at auction by a previous ambassador — and a brass Buddha. To be sure, the residence abounds in Swedish glassware, chandeliers, and royal portraits as well. Above the entrance door is the Swedish coat of arms with its distinctive three crowns — representing the Scandinavian kingdoms of Sweden, Denmark, and Norway, which were united for more than 120 years, beginning with a treaty signed in the Swedish city of Kalmar in 1397. Superseding the trio of crowns is the larger royal diadem of King Erik of Pomerania, overall ruler of the Nordic union.

The Swedes, who bought the house from Lawrence in 1950, know that unexpected contrasts are endemic to a nation that stretches from Baltic ports to Lapland, where the first snow may fall in August and the last in early June. The change of seasons alone is a matter for wonderment, and at no other embassy is the coming of spring — marked by the April 30 Feast of Valborg — so ebulliently toasted, with a paean to the distant and budding Virginia hills on the other side of the Potomac River.

The Swedes serve up some of diplomatic Washington's most anticipated cuisine, prepared by the chef in his own small house off the walled garden. A smorgasbord might offer a choice among such national dishes as jellied pig's feet, reindeer meat, goose-blood soup, or sour herring, which, a Swedish Institute handbook, *Traditional Festivities in Sweden,* points out, results from "controlled rotting" of the fish after their hermetically sealed tins have turned "distinctly 'swollen' by the time they are ready for sale." Sardonically, the author adds, "A pungent aroma — delectable to some, repulsive to others — fills the room whenever a can is opened." When the Christmas gnome is about, a stack of deep-fried Swedish rosettes, drenched in powdered sugar, makes up for any indignity.

If the mind plays tricks at the Royal Swedish embassy, so do the Swedes, for whom practical jokes are a delicious diversion. Only in Sweden would an entire television network attempt to fool the nation into believing it could turn its black-and-white television sets into color models by stretching nylon hosiery over the screens. To the owners of thousands of ruined stockings on that Första April, the network announced, "April Fool!" It's a bit like the sensation one gets opening the door of the hacienda on Nebraska Avenue any night of the year and finding the pragmatic people who represent what Marquis Childs once called "Sweden, the middle way."

94

RESIDENCE OF THE
AMBASSADOR OF TURKEY

The Everett House
1606 23rd Street, Northwest
George Oakley Totten, Jr., Architect

1915

IF EVER THERE WAS MUSIC TO AN ARCHITECT'S
ears, it was the words uttered in 1914 by multimillionaire Edward Ham-
lin Everett when he commissioned George Oakley Totten to build a
home on Sheridan Circle: "Cost is no object! And style and design are
up to you."

Everett earned his walking-around money in Texas oil and Missouri beer, but he made his fortune on his patent for the simple crimped
cap that sealed millions of bottles of that beer, and soft drinks, from
coast to coast at a time when almost every American city had at least
one brewery. The "Bottle-Top King" had met Totten through Everett's
friends the Hendersons at the time the architect was helping Mary
Foote Henderson turn upper 16th Street into Embassy Row.

Ironically, Totten had spent time in Constantinople, where he
was about to embark on another dream commission as Sultan Abdul-
Hamid II's personal architect—just as the Young Turk rebellion
brought down the Ottoman ruler—so Totten returned to Washington
and built mansions for Mary Henderson instead.

On the site of a former city dump, the brick and Bowling Green
granite home he designed had architectural details from three centuries.
The "cost is no object" imprint was clearly evident in the ornate ball-

National hero Mustafa
Kemal Atatürk's bust
looms on a landing.
Opposite:
"Bottle-Top King"
Edward Everett told
his architect
to damn the cost for
his new mansion.
Following page:
Vases add color
to the building's stone-
walled sunroom.

room with coffered ceiling, and the house's stained-glass bays, hand-carved staircase, billiard room, velvet-covered walls, teakwood floors, basement swimming pool, and roof garden with a spectacular view of the city. Many exterior details, from the fluted columns to ornate portico, suggest homes Totten saw during his stay on the Bosporus.

The "Bottle-Top King" met operatic soprano Grace Burnap at a Henderson party in 1919 and married her. According to Henry Mitchell's *Houses of the Capital,* the Everetts entertained lavishly and were famous for their gala "Evenings with Music" at which Grace and other opera stars performed.

Everett lived in his new mansion until his death in 1929; Grace stayed on three years more. In 1932 the Republic of Turkey leased the house with the prospect of buying it, although Henderson was dangling one of her uptown castles before the Turks as well. A year or so later they opted to stay where they were, buying the Everett mansion and all its furnishings, adding over the years their own Turkish rugs, crystal, and a gigantic bronze head of the republic's founder, Mustafa Kemal Atatürk.

The irony was complete: Turks would live in a spectacular George Oakley Totten house after all.

In 1955, long after the house had become the Turkish embassy, Ambassador Haydar Gork almost literally stumbled on the swimming pool, which had been boarded over by an earlier delegation. He unsealed it, had fluorescent lights installed overhead, and painted the walls and ceilings. "Not that the Turkish Embassy needs the luxury of a swimming pool," Ambassador Gork told Evelyn Peyton Gordon of the *Washington Daily News.* "But since it is there, why not use it!"

IT WAS NATURAL, IN 1939, FOR REPRESENTATIVES of the Vatican to turn to architect Frank Vernon Murphy to create a dignified new diplomatic mission on Massachusetts Avenue's Observatory Circle. Murphy, chairman of the architecture department at Catholic University in Washington, had designed several structures on that campus, as well as church buildings for several denominations from Baltimore to Toledo.

The new nunciature—then called the Apostolic Delegation—was built 10 years after the Italian government recognized the sovereignty of the Holy See and created the independent state of Vatican City. The Vatican had owned the Massachusetts Avenue lot since 1931. Murphy's creation is a three-story Italian Renaissance palazzo of Indiana limestone on a granite base, with a tile roof. It cost $550,000 to build and furnish, and to help pay for it, the *New York Times* noted, "each Catholic diocese in the United States has been assessed according to its resources." The garden courtyard features the bronze Pigna Fountain, in the shape of a fir cone, a one-third-scale reproduction of that in the Cortile della Pigna in the Vatican Museum in Rome.

Murphy, who incorporated stained glass liberally throughout the building, described it as "frankly inspired from the more restrained and dignified of the Italian palaces of the Renaissance." European travelers compared it with the Villa d'Este on Lake Como and the Villa Medici in Rome. One stained-glass window, transported from the mission's cramped Biltmore Street residence, depicts scenes and texts from the "Paradise" section of Dante's *Divine Comedy*. Portraits of popes, cardinals, and saints, including Mother Elizabeth Ann Seton, the first native-born American to be canonized, hang throughout the house. Secular figures, including George Washington and Christopher Columbus, have their places as well.

The nunciature sits across the street from the vice president's residence, catercorner from the British embassy and next door to the Norwegian diplomatic residence. For two decades it was also a neighbor of the "Texas embassy," home of Representative Clark Thompson and his wife, Libby, whose regal entertaining nearly always included priests from the nunciature. In 1991 Finland purchased the Thompson home for $6 million and demolished it to make room for the newest Massachusetts Avenue embassy.

The apostolic delegate who took up residence in Murphy's new edifice, Archbishop Pietro Fumasino Biondi, was described as the "all but official" ambassador, for no diplomatic relations existed between Washington and Vatican City at the time. Officially the mission served instead as a link between American dioceses and the Holy See. Relations had been in hiatus since 1878, when the Italian government absorbed the Papal States into a new, unified Italy. Washington did not resume formal recognition until 1983, after more than 100 other nations had already done so. William A. Wilson was sent as U.S. ambassador to the Holy See; Archbishop Pio Laghi, upon presenting his papers to President Ronald Reagan early the next year, became the pronuncio, while the legation took on the designation "Apostolic Nunciature."

APOSTOLIC NUNCIATURE
OF THE HOLY SEE
(THE VATICAN)
3339 Massachusetts Avenue, Northwest
Frederick Vernon Murphy, Architect
1939

The organization Americans United for Separation of Church and State, two Protestant denominations, and a Catholic lay group filed suit to block diplomatic relations, saying such ties would give preference to "one religious denomination over all others" and thereby violate the First Amendment. Supporters pointed out that an informal diplomatic relationship already existed: George Washington had sent a consul to the Holy See in 1797; James K. Polk had upgraded the office to legation status in 1867; and several U.S. ministers to the Holy See had been confirmed by the Senate. The United States also had diplomatic relations with the Court of St. James, even though the monarch was head of the Church of England, the Justice Department noted, and the United States and the Holy See had routinely signed international treaties and agreements. Plaintiffs countered by pointing to a speech by Archbishop Laghi, in which he said that the Holy See's authority is spiritual and moral and not dependent upon temporal power. The U.S. government responded that "however the Holy See views itself, it is a highly influential player on the stage of world diplomacy." As a diplomatic player, the nunciature serves as a conduit for information between the Holy See and the U.S. government, as well as the liaison between Roman Catholic churches here and the Vatican.

In accepting an honorary degree from Catholic University in 1984, Archbishop Laghi pointed to the remarks of Pope Paul VI when he served as pro-secretary of state before his elevation: "If diplomacy works through the medium of responsible representatives, if it seeks to construct peace, if it is indeed the art of peace, then no other institution and no other relationship between the peoples more deserves the support of the Catholic Church which, more than any other earthly good, seeks, preaches and gives birth to this peace, true peace."

The marble fountain in the Nunciature's rear courtyard copies a larger one at the Vatican.
Opposite: Stained glass depicts scenes from Dante's
DIVINE COMEDY.

Archibishop Agostino Cacciavillan, pronuncio to the United States in 1991, reflected on the subject as well: "The art of diplomacy, after all, has everything to do with honest exchange and frank encounter. It does not seek confrontation, but it relies on mutual understanding and is at pains to protect the integrity of that dialog which is the special bond of friendship between those countries which exchange ambassadors. Once you admit that diplomacy exists to promote peace, justice, and mutual cooperation, it seems so natural that the Catholic Church, founded by the Prince of Peace, would have such a venerable and effective posture in world diplomacy."

════╕╓║╖╒════

RESIDENCE OF THE
AMBASSADOR
OF VENEZUELA

2443 Massachusetts Avenue, Northwest

Chester A. Patterson, Architect

════ *1939* ════

THE VENEZUELAN EMBASSY HAS BEEN THE SCENE
of dozens of memorable affairs—masquerade balls, elegant dinners, and
receptions—but none more memorable than its first. In 1939 the United
States and Venezuela established full diplomatic relations for the first
time. In February 1940 Don Diogenes Escalante, the first ambassador
of Venezuela, opened the doors of his new official residence for a
housewarming. As the *Washington Times-Herald*'s scribe Jean Eliot
wrote, the ambassador and his wife "had asked 1,200 guests between
the hours of 5 and 8 o'clock. Seemingly none sent regrets, most of them
arrived along about 6 o'clock, and the most spectacular traffic jam ever
seen at an embassy party was the result." A line of 300 or more people
snaked down the driveway on foot to Massachusetts Avenue, as visitors were caught in a bottleneck created by the new embassy's narrow
doorway. It was "like the woman who bought shoes too small for her
feet to look elegant," sniffed *Times-Herald* columnist Igor Cassini. "But
you've got to suffer to be beautiful!"

The crush was exacerbated as hats and coats were tucked into
dumbwaiters on both sides of the tiny foyer, using a system copied from
the Hotel Savoy in London, to be dropped to a cloakroom below. (The
Washington Post was unimpressed with these "robot hat-checkers, the
very latest gadgets for ultra-modern living. . . . The guests were too fast,
and the dumbwaiters were too slow.") In line, the German envoy
bumped into the Australian minister, but no talk of the ongoing war was
overheard. The chief of protocol, George Summerlin, was caught between the comers and the goers, Cassini reported, "and it required all
his long experience of diplomatc ceremonials to get out of the place
alive, but not without having crushed some innocent feet."

Inside, orchids by the hundreds from the Venezuelan jungles
had been flown in for the affair. Cassini spotted the French ambassador,
"who could not even raise his arm to arrange his mustache, due to the
crowd." Dancing to Barnee's Orchestra, cork-popping, drinks of
"whiskey and soda on tap" were had by many.

Ambassador Escalante described the $200,000 residence, de-
signed by New York architect Chester A. Patterson, as "a house, not a
palace." The building's wide expanse of windows outside, likened at the
time to a pavilion at the previous year's New York World's Fair, was inside married to Venezuelan touches with pleasing effect. A solarium was
added in 1965, and a covered swimming pool was built on the east side
of the house in 1967.

At the time of the building's housewarming, *Washington Daily
News* writer Evelyn Peyton Gordon described the 20-room concrete
structure, covered in white stucco, as "semi-modern." The residence as
well as the chancery annex on California Street—the first to be built by
a Latin American nation in Washington—did not suggest Venezuela,
and both buildings were certainly a departure from the ornate style fa-
vored along Embassy Row. The triangular lot, purchased from several
owners, covers two-thirds of an acre.

The American legation in Caracas and the new Venezuelan
diplomatic presence in Washington were elevated at this time to the

status of embassies, the latter moving from a 16th Street apartment.

The house features a huge salon, a downstairs game room, and a library paneled in Venezuelan mahogany, with carved scrolls symbolizing the nation's agriculture, literature, and justice. Flower gardens surround the building on three sides. The residence includes many paintings, such as Pedro Centano's *The Three Races,* which depicts three graceful nudes representing Venezuela's ethnic diversity. The ambassador's wife, Georgiana Gonzalez, admitted to a visitor in 1953 that the provocative painting draws considerable comment. "We found it tucked away in the cellar when we came here and immediately rehung it," she told the *Daily News.* "Most people enjoy it—except those who sit with their backs to the picture. One guest suggested [hanging] an opposite mirror; he had a stiff neck at the end of dinner because he turned constantly to join the comment!"

Centano also painted the striking panels of the nation's historical heroes, including Simon Bolívar and Guaicaipuro, a native South American who fought valiantly against the Spanish occupiers.

*Venezuela has filled
its ambassador's
residence with classicist
and abstract artwork—
and some that is
controversial.
Following pages:
The unadorned, white
stucco building departed
from most of the
city's richly wrought
diplomatic buildings.*

Further Reading

BOOKS

Applewhite, E. J. *Washington Itself.* New York: Alfred A. Knopf, 1961.

Cox, Warren J., Hugh Newell Jacobsen, Francis D. Lethbridge, and David R. Rosenthal. *A Guide to the Architecture of Washington, D.C.,* 2nd ed. New York: McGraw-Hill, 1974.

Eig, Emily Hotaling. "Kalorama: Two Centuries of Beautiful Views." In *Washington at Home,* Kathryn Schneider Smith, ed. Washington, D.C.: Windsor Publications, 1988.

Goode, James M. *Capital Losses: A Cultural History of Washington's Destroyed Buildings.* Washington, D.C.: Smithsonian Institution Press, 1979.

Goodwill Embassy Tour and Gala programs, 1947–91 (written in recent years by Allison Brown). Washington, D.C.: Davis Memorial Goodwill Industries.

Hammond, John Hays. *The Autobiography of John Hays Hammond,* 2 vols. New York: Farrar & Rinehard, 1935.

Highsmith, Carol, and Ted Landphair. *Pennsylvania Avenue: America's Main Street.* Washington, D.C.: American Institute of Architects Press, 1988.

Kreysa, Peter. *Diplomatic Dishes: A Cook's Tour of the Embassies.* Washington, D.C.: Maehlmann Press, 1989.

Kohler, Sue A., and Jeffrey R. Carson. *Sixteenth Street Architecture,* vols. 1 and 2. Washington, D.C.: Commission of Fine Arts, 1978.

Jennings, J. L., Jr., Sue A. Kohler, and Jeffrey R. Carson. *Massachusetts Avenue Architecture,* vols. 1 and 2. Washington, D.C.: Commission of Fine Arts, 1973, 1975.

McLean, Evalyn Walsh, with Boyden Sparkes. *Father Struck It Rich.* New York: Little, Brown, 1936.

Miller, Hope Ridings. Photographs by Charles Baptie. *Great Houses of Washington, D.C.* New York: C. N. Potter, 1969.

Miller, Hope Ridings. *Embassy Row: The Life & Times of Diplomatic Washington.* New York: Holt, Rinehart and Winston, 1969.

Mitchell, Henry. Photographs by Derry Moore. *Washington: Houses of the Capital.* New York: Viking Press, 1982.

Smith, A. Robert, and Eric Sevareid. *Washington: Magnificent Capital.* Garden City, N.Y.: Doubleday, 1965.

W.P.A. Guide to Washington, D.C. Federal Writers' Project of the Works Progress Administration for the District of Columbia. New York: Pantheon Books, 1942.

MAGAZINE ARTICLES, REPORTS, AND PAMPHLETS

Andrus, Patrick. "Sheridan-Kalorama Historic District: Evaluation of Potential National Significance" (report). Washington, D.C.: U.S. Department of the Interior, National Park Service, October 30, 1989.

"Comprehensive Plan for the National Capital." In "Foreign Missions and International Organizations" chapter and "Federal Elements" map supplement. Washington, D.C.: National Capital Planning Commission, 1978.

Conroy, Sarah Booth. "The Era of Elegant Embassies." *Washington Post Potomac* magazine, January 25, 1976.

"The Embassy of Venezuela." Report by the Embassy's Information Service. Washington, D.C., 1970.

Fawcett, Waldon. "Envoys at Washington." *The Cosmopolitan,* May 1901.

Forbes, Quinn. "The British Embassy." *The Illustrated American,* November 28, 1896.

"Foreign Missions and International Organizations: Real Property Manual." Washington, D.C.: U.S. Department of State, 1987.

"History of the Residence of the South African Ambassador in Washington, D.C." Undated publication of the embassy of the Republic of South Africa.

"India's Corner of Washington." *Washington Post Potomac* magazine, October 20, 1968.

"Indonesian Embassy: Nomination to the National Register of Historic Places." Washington, D.C.: U.S. Department of the Interior, National Park Service, 1989.

Laghi, Archibishop Pio. "The True Nature of Papal Diplomacy." *Origins,* May 3, 1984.

"Massachusetts Avenue Historical District: Nomination to the National Register of Historic Places." Washington, D.C.: U.S. Department of the Interior, National Park Service, 1989.

McLellan, Diana. "Perfect Pitch: With Charm, Intelligence, and a Very Good Resumé, Henry Catto Is the Man for the Job—Almost Any Job." *Washingtonian,* August 1991.

"National Capital Landmarks." Recommendation to the National Capital Planning Commission and the Commission of Fine Arts. Washington, D.C.: Joint Committee on Landmarks, November 8, 1964.

"Old English" (Garrett House). *House and Garden,* September 1937.

Radlovic, Monty. "Iron Curtain Diplomats in Washington." *The Diplomat,* November 1952.

Reese, Thomas J., S.J. "Diplomatic Relations with the Vatican." *America,* March 16, 1985.

Shalett, Sidney. "Washington's Diplomatic Whirl." *Better Homes & Gardens,* October 1958.

"Sheraton-Kalorama Historical District: Nomination to the National Register of Historic Places." Washington, D.C.: U.S. Department of the Interior, National Park Service, 1989.

Spatz, Frances, and William Engle. "Magnificent Mary." *The American Weekly,* February 27, 1949.

Tully, Andrew. "Kremlin, U.S.A." *Collier's,* August 20, 1954.

"U.S.-Soviet Agreement on Embassy Construction in Washington. Public Information Series, U.S. Department of State, Bureau of Public Affairs, May 19, 1987.

Wood, Junius. "The World Beats a Path to our Doorstep." *Nation's Business,* August 1945.

EMBASSIES OF WASHINGTON WAS DESIGNED BY Rebecca S. Neimark of Meadows & Wiser, Washington, D.C. The text was set in Cochin, a typeface designed by Deberney & Peignot in 1910 as part of the revival of Renaissance-style typefaces in the early 20th century. The italic and display type was set in Bernhard, a face designed by Lucian Bernhard in 1937. The book was produced using Quark Xpress and Adobe Illustrator software on an Apple Macintosh computer. Page mechanicals were output by General Typographers, Inc., of Washington, D.C., and the book was printed through Palace Press, of Singapore.

THE
TREE DOCTOR

A GUIDE TO
TREE CARE AND MAINTENANCE

DAN PRENDERGAST AND ERIN PRENDERGAST

FIREFLY BOOKS

A FIREFLY BOOK

Published by Firefly Books (U.S.) Inc. 2003

First Printing

PUBLISHER CATALOGING IN PUBLICATION DATA (U.S.)
(Library of Congress Standards)

Prendergast, Daniel.
    The tree doctor : a guide to tree care and maintenance / Daniel Prendergast ; and Erin Prendergast.—1st ed.
[144] p. : col. ill. , photos. ; cm.
Includes index.
Summary: A comprehensive guide to everything a tree owner needs to know about planting and maintaining trees.
ISBN 1-55297-741-2
ISBN 1-55297-742-0 (pbk.)
1. Trees, Care of. 2. Ornamental trees—Diseases and pests. I. Prendergast, Erin. II. Title.
635.9/ 77 21   SB435.A75 2003

Published in the United States in 2003 by
Firefly Books (U.S.) Inc.
P.O. Box 1338, Ellicott Station
Buffalo, New York, USA
14205

Published in Canada in 2003 by Key Porter Books Limited.

Electronic formatting: Jean Lightfoot Peters

Illustration: John Lightfoot

All photographs by the author, unless otherwise noted.

Printed and bound in Spain

CONTENTS

We dedicate this book to our parents and siblings,
and to all those who love trees.

Chapter 1
THE BENEFITS OF TREES

For many of us, trees are a constant force in our lives. They flourish in our backyards, city streets, and neighborhood parks, lending an air of humble nobility to the frenetic pace of our daily routines. In northern climates, the changing characteristics of deciduous trees signal the arrival of new seasons, when blazing foliage of red, orange, and yellow leaves sheds with the approach of winter, and fresh **buds** and green growth appear during spring, a time of renewed life. In the south, the live oak is a popular and characteristic shade tree, stately and vibrant all year long. Numerous species throughout Canada and the United States, such as the giant Douglas fir of the Pacific Northwest, the flowering magnolia of the Deep South, and the syrup-producing sugar maple of the Northeast are cherished symbols of home, valued for their distinct features, their strength, and their beauty.

The International Society of Arboriculture, the largest and most influential organization of its kind, serves the tree care industry as a scientific and educational organization. The ISA has published a brochure on the benefits of trees, which are outlined in this chapter.

Tree owners know that the impact of trees on a landscape transcends their size and stature. Trees make life pleasant for us, and have social benefits.

Time spent under a shade tree on a hot summer day is peaceful—and also cooler. Air is cooled as it moves through the tree's canopy.

Homeowners can reverse the effects of the city as a heat island by planting more trees and increasing the urban forest cover. This helps make our cities more livable, and it protects the health of residents. If you're concerned about the environment, you can make a difference by planting a tree. Many cities throughout North America encourage community commitment to trees. Learn more about planting in your area by contacting local municipal representatives, or visit on-line resources such as The National Arbor Day Foundation/Tree City USA website: www.arborday.org, or the City of Toronto's Tree Advocacy Program website: www.city.toronto.on.ca/parks/treeadvocacy.htm. Toronto promotes a Tree Advocacy Program to encourage citizens to improve the quality of life for themselves and future generations. Although in its infancy, the Tree Advocacy Program has planted tens of thousands of trees at more than forty-five sites to maintain and improve Toronto's urban forest canopy. The city, among others throughout North America, will plant trees for free on the city-owned portion of your front lawn.

Trees are hardy companions, lasting for lifetimes, even generations.

The urban forests in ravines, parks, and residential neighborhoods help improve the quality of city life for all inhabitants.

Time spent amidst a grove of trees is often relaxing. While painters and writers have been inspired by the aesthetic and spiritual appeal of trees, hospital patients have been known to recover from surgery more quickly when their rooms offered views of trees. The strong ties between people and trees are evident in the resistance of community residents to removing trees to widen streets, and in the valiant efforts of individuals to save large or historic trees. Trees benefit our communities by bringing groups together in neighborhood plantings. We often become personally attached to trees.

And why not? Trees are fun—no play equipment will ever replace a good climbing tree. Trees add color, form, and dimension to our gardens. They are our steadfast companions, lasting for lifetimes.

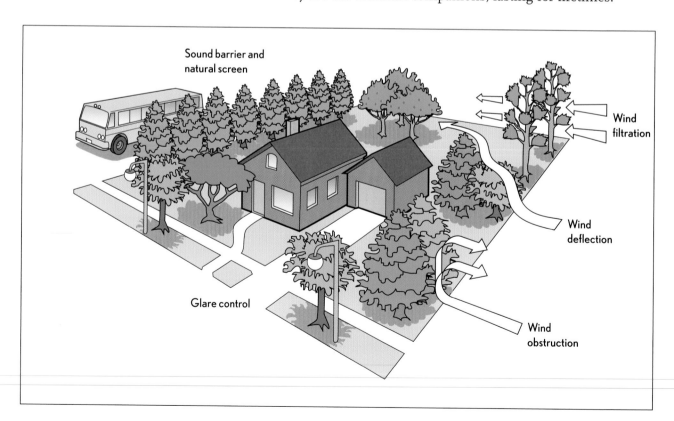

Sound barrier and natural screen

Wind filtration

Wind deflection

Wind obstruction

Glare control

Because of their potential for long life, trees are frequently planted as living memorials, establishing links to our past. Among Earth's longest-lived and largest organisms, many trees can last one to two hundred years, or even longer. The eastern hemlock, for example, can live six hundred to one thousand years. Even smaller trees, considered short-lived, typically survive sixty to eighty years.

In addition to providing social benefits, trees alter the environment in which we live by moderating the climate, improving air quality, conserving water, and providing refuge to wildlife. Radiant energy

Trees help make our city streets more aesthetically pleasing and natural looking.

The combined chemistry of the thousands of leaves on each tree eliminates an enormous amount of pollution from the air. Leaves absorb air pollutants such as ozone, carbon monoxide, and sulfur dioxide.

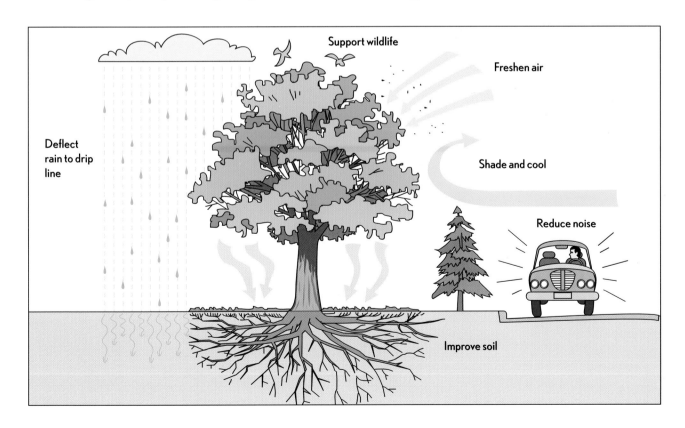

Support wildlife

Freshen air

Deflect rain to drip line

Shade and cool

Reduce noise

Improve soil

Trees help prevent soil erosion in hills and ravines and along waterways. In addition, trees support an underground network of life, which helps keep the soil around them healthy.

On average, woody plants add between 5 and 7 percent to the value of a residential lot.

from the sun is absorbed or deflected by leaves on deciduous trees in the summer and is filtered by their branches during the winter. Trees also combat wind speed—the more compact the foliage on the trees or group of trees, the greater the influence of the windbreak—and have an impressive ability to muffle noise. Leaves and small branches act as baffles, absorbing and deflecting sound. The downward fall of rain is diverted by trees. Trees intercept water and store some of it, thereby reducing storm runoff and the possibility of flooding.

Leaves filter the air we breathe by removing dust and other particles. Leaves absorb carbon dioxide from the air to form carbohydrates that are used in the woody plants' structure and function. In this process, leaves also absorb other air pollutants such as ozone, carbon monoxide, and sulfur dioxide. The combined chemistry of the thousands of leaves on each tree eliminates an enormous volume of pollutants from the air. After processing all the chemicals, trees give off water and oxygen.

A mature maple or oak tree transpires 82 gallons of moisture every twenty-four hours. A great redwood will transpire approximately 500 gallons of moisture a day. This moisture eventually takes the form of dew or rain. Trees draw upon the deep

In addition to offering shade for animals, farmers also often plant trees in their fields to create windbreaks, which reduce wind and soil erosion.

The presence of trees on residential lots brings life and energy to paved streets.

By planting trees in our cities, we help create a more natural environment. Birds and other wildlife are attracted to the area. Natural cycles of plant growth, reproduction, and decomposition are present, both above and below ground. Harmony and balance are restored to the urban landscape.

groundwater, thereby lifting water tables and maintaining moisture in the surrounding topsoil.

Even below the ground, trees are doing beneficial things for the landscape. Tree roots anchor the tree in the ground, soak up water and nutrients from the soil, prevent soil from eroding, and support an underground universe of beneficial insects and organisms, which, in turn, keep all the soil around them healthy and teeming with life.

Trees are efficient at cooling the air. The air cools as water vapor from leaves evaporates, which explains why it feels fresh and cool under a tree on a hot day.

Shade trees are tremendous assets for urban communities. When the sun beats down on barren concrete, asphalt, and glass, cities heat up to nine degrees Fahrenheit warmer than their rural counterparts,

Trees harbor wildlife, and attract birds to your garden.

creating a phenomenon known as the heat island effect. Since such surfaces retain heat, they stay hotter for longer periods of time. After sunset, these hot surfaces continue to radiate stored heat back into the atmosphere well into the evening, making it feel warmer than outside city limits.

Shade trees can cool individual neighborhoods and entire cities by preventing the heat island effect in two ways: in the heat of summer, temperatures are ten degrees Fahrenheit cooler under the shade of a mature tree, and as wind moves air through a shade canopy, it is

The benefits of trees are impressive and far-reaching:

- ► **Social**. Trees have the power to quiet our souls, and to connect us to one another. They add civility to the harsh environs of urban life.
- ► **Environment**. Trees cool and clean the air, deflect wind, muffle noise, and improve soil conditions.
- ► **Economic**. Trees help decrease electricity bills, and increase the value of real estate.

cooled. A stand of trees, therefore, can create a welcoming oasis effect.

Trees planted effectively will also help you save money and conserve energy. One of the best means of energy conservation is through the planting of windbreaks. Living windbreaks of trees can do much to keep our soil productive and improve our environment, in addition to reducing or eliminating the undesirable effects of excessive wind velocities.

The direct economic benefits provided by trees are usually associated with energy costs. By providing good protection from winds, trees can reduce winter heating costs and summer cooling costs by 25 to 30 percent. Trees also provide indirect economic benefits to communities. For example, customers will receive lower electricity bills when power companies use less water in their cooling towers, build fewer new facilities to meet peak demands, use reduced amounts of fossil fuel in their furnaces, and need to take fewer measures to control air pollution. Communities also save money when fewer facilities are built to control storm water in the region.

Trees in public spaces add dignity and natural beauty to city life, all year round.

Trees have a considerable impact on the value of real estate. Healthy, mature trees can add as much as 20 percent or more to the value of a residential property. Studies show that people are willing to pay 3 to 7 percent more for a house in a well-treed neighborhood. According to the ISA, property values of landscaped homes are 5 to 20 percent higher than those of non-landscaped homes.

Municipal trees often serve several architectural and engineering functions. They provide privacy, emphasize views or screen out unsightly ones, reduce glare and reflection, and direct pedestrian traffic. Their presence complements and enhances buildings and architectural features, much to the delight of city dwellers.

In addition to the material benefits that trees bestow upon urban centers and city inhabitants are the ways in which woody plants enhance the look of residential homes. The use of trees in gardens and landscaped settings provides the opportunity to create, sustain, and enjoy an earthly paradise in our own backyard. Perhaps the greatest benefit offered by trees is the view from a window!

Chapter 2
TREE SELECTION AND PLACEMENT

Trees establish a landscape's general character more than any other plants. They are the most dominant and permanent elements in our yards, and can determine the framework of our garden by dictating the amount of sun or shade that enters the space. Trees are awesome landmarks. They can direct sightlines and create perspective. Trees can soften hard architectural lines and link structures to the landscape. They can be used to frame special vistas and black out unattractive ones. Trees can also offer seasonal features such as bright spring blossoms, showy flowers or fruits, and blazing autumn foliage. A balance of evergreen and deciduous trees provides variety of color and texture throughout the seasons. When carefully placed, trees can block or divert prevailing winds, and absorb or moderate noises outside.

Fortunately, the range of trees available to gardeners is impressive—there are scores of striking tree types from which to choose.

Trees can direct sight lines and create perspective.

What is a tree?

A tree, simply defined, is a tall woody plant, usually with a single trunk supporting a distinct crown of foliage. (A shrub is also a woody plant, usually smaller, and has branches at ground level. Trees are longer-lived than most shrubs.) Trees fall into two basic categories categories: evergreen, those that have green foliage throughout the year, and deciduous, those that lose their leaves in fall.

What is the difference between a tree and a shrub? Both are woody plants, but shrubs are usually smaller, have branches at ground level, and are multi-stemmed. Trees live longer than shrubs.

Trees offer seasonal focal points such as showy blossoms and autumn foliage color.

Evergreen

Evergreen trees and shrubs keep their foliage year-round. Most evergreens, such as pine, spruce, and fir trees, have needles. However, there are also evergreens with broad leaves, and evergreens with scale-like leaves, such as cedars and junipers. Trees such as pine, spruce, and cedar that produce their seeds within cones are called **conifers**. Male cones produce pollen, which blows on the wind to female cones. Once the pollen is shed, the male cones fall. Seeds develop within female cones, which can remain on trees for more than three years. Most conifers are evergreens, although there are some exceptions.

Deciduous

Trees and shrubs that shed all of their foliage during autumn to prepare for dormancy during winter are deciduous. (There are some exceptions, such as the larch, which is referred to as a deciduous conifer, a cone-bearing tree that sheds its soft needles in fall, after a display of brilliant yellow foliage.) Large deciduous trees are commonly referred to as **shade trees**.

A balance of evergreen and deciduous trees offers year-round interest for the homeowner.

Most trees reach 50 to 80 feet in height, but some grow taller. For example, the eastern white pine can reach 100 feet; the American sycamore, tulip tree, and white oak can reach 115 feet. Small trees such as the pussy willow, mountain maple, and poison sumac rarely exceed 16 feet. To support large trunks and branches, many cells are gradually transformed into non-living tissues, such as wood and cork. These dead cells account for approximately 80 percent of a mature tree. The remaining 20 percent comprises live cells that maintain vital functions.

The term **dwarf** refers to trees smaller than the usual size for a particular species. A tree variety that grows to 10 feet tall may be considered a dwarf if the usual height of that tree species is much larger. Dwarf varieties grow slowly, only a few inches each year.

What parts make up a tree?

- The sturdy, woody **trunk** of a tree supports the weight of the mass aboveground, and supplies its living tissues with water and nutrients from the ground and with food from the leaves.
- A trunk is made up of several distinct layers, each with a different function.
- The outermost layer is the **bark**, which forms a protective, waterproof layer that can shield the tree from fire damage, insect or fungal attack, and stress from sudden temperature changes.
- All bark has small, round or elongated pores called **lenticels**, which allow the trunk to breathe.

A tree's roots serve four primary functions: anchorage, storage, absorption, and conduction. Roots grow near the surface where moisture and oxygen are available. This is usually in the top 8 to 12 inches of soil. Roots extend outward horizontally from the tree great distances, often one to two times the height of the tree itself.

Absorbing roots are the smaller roots with fine root hairs, which help in the uptake of water and minerals. The downward-growing **tap root** of young trees is usually choked out by expansion of roots around it or is diverted by unfavorable growing conditions. **Feeder roots** compete directly with the roots of grass and other groundcovers, and provide the major portion of the absorption surface of a tree's root system

Many trees have fungi called **mycorrhizae** on their roots. This fungi covers the root hairs and helps with the absorption process. In turn, the mycorrhizae are fed by the tree roots, forming a symbiotic relationship.

- Bark cells grow from a special thin layer of living cells on the inner side of the bark, called **cork** or **bark cambium**.
- Each year cork cambium lays down successive layer of bark. As growth continues, the outermost layers of bark are forced to split into ridges or scales, or peel away (like birch bark).
- To the inner side of the cork cambium lies the **phloem**. This thin layer of cells is very important because it carries food (in the form of carbohydrates) produced by the leaves to all other living tissues.
- On the inner side of the phloem lies an even narrower ring of cells called the **cambium**. These cells are responsible for increases in the diameters of trunks or branches.
- Cambium cells produce phloem cells along the outer surface of the ring and **xylem** cells along the inner surface. The xylem cells

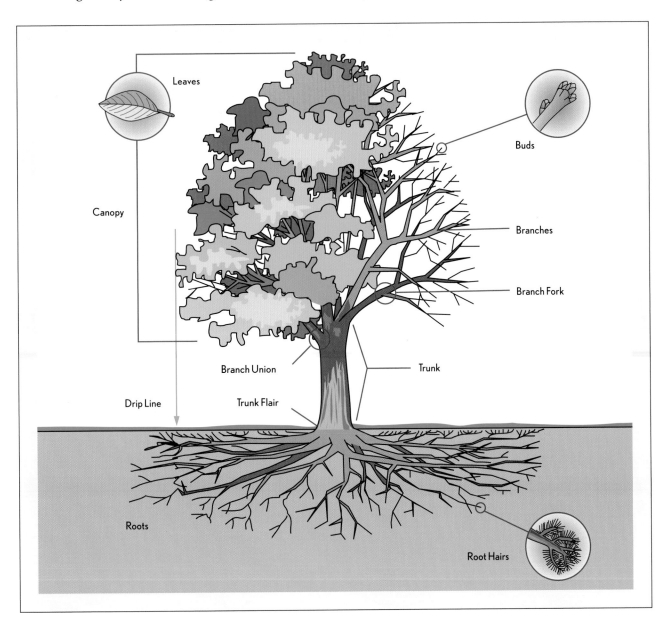

transport water, nutrients, and oxygen up from the roots to the branches and leaves, where the tree produces food for energy. The cells join and form thousands of elongated capillary tubes that extend up the trunk.

- Most of the rest of the trunk, referred to as wood, is made up of dead xylem cells. As long as xylem cells continue to transport fluids, they are part of the tree's **sapwood**, but once they clog and cease to function, they become part of **heartwood**.

- Heartwood helps support the trunk, but a tree's heartwood can rot away, leaving hollow trunk, while branches and leaves continue to flourish.

- Trees growing in temperate regions, where there are definite seasonal changes in growth, develop patterns in their wood called **annual rings**—the rings of wood laid down each year after the burst of spring growth.

- Annual rings may be observed as concentric circles across a log or stump when a tree is cut down, or as a series of light and dark bands. Counting such rings reveals the age of the tree.

- We can learn about a tree's history and growth rate because health and environment factors affect ring widths. For example, drought, cold years, insect infestations, and pollution can all make a tree produce narrow annual rings. Increased light and warm years can result in wider rings.

- **Branches** develop the same woody structure as trunks. Young shoots and branches are called **twigs**.

- In twigs, the soft central cone of early growth, called the **pith**, is more obvious.

- Branch tips and twigs grow lengthwise as well as widthwise (although a branch at 3 feet in height will always be 3 feet at

Look for healthy green leaves and bud development.

Make sure the trunk, or main stem of the tree, appears healthy and has not suffered any damage from transport.

height). Recent growth is often shown in leaf or bud scars on young branches. Each summer, small branches produce buds along their lengths and tips. By autumn, each bud contains the rudimentary cells necessary to produce a new structure.

- The tip bud is often much larger than lower side-buds or lateral buds. It produces a new extension of the shoot the following year.
- **Leaves** house the food factories and respiration devices of the tree.
- A tree produces food by first capturing the sun's energy with the green pigment **chlorophyll**, concentrated in outer leaf tissues.

A glossary of terms is provided at the back of this book. Here, various terms such as V-shaped crotch and central leader, are defined in more detail. Please refer to the glossary when you come across a term that requires clarification.

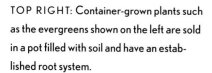

TOP RIGHT: Container-grown plants such as the evergreens shown on the left are sold in a pot filled with soil and have an established root system.

ABOVE: Balled-and-burlapped trees are sold with their roots surrounded with a ball of soil wrapped in burlap. They are generally heavy to lift, so you might consider an additional expense of delivery and planting assistance.

RIGHT: The root ball should be solid and well supported with wire or twine. (The circle indicates a V-shaped crotch, something to avoid.)

- A leaf then uses the trapped energy in a process called **photosynthesis**, which is the combining of carbon dioxide and water to produce sugars and oxygen.
- Leaves take in carbon dioxide and give off moisture and oxygen through their stomata, tiny pores in the leaves.

How to choose a healthy tree from a nursery

To ensure that the tree you buy will be successful on your property when planted, select a vigorous tree. A tree purchased in poor health will likely have more problems, attract insects, and require more maintenance. Here are some important signs to look for when choosing a tree, as suggested by the ISA:

1. Avoid trees with damage to the trunk or broken branches that have been injured in transport or from equipment.
2. Look for good twig extension growth, which indicates the plant is healthy.
3. Avoid trees with V-shaped crotches, poor branch spacing, and upright branches (page 28, circled).
4. Look for an abundance of healthy green leaves.
5. The tree should have one central leader with spreading branches. Do not purchase a tree that has two competing leaders.
6. Look for insects and disease problems on the leaves, branches, and trunk.
7. The root ball should be solid and well supported within twine or a wire basket. The ball should be moist and protected from drying out.
8. The roots should be white. Roots that are brown or black indicate poor health. Avoid trees with roots that are circling, kinked, or girdling other roots.

How trees are sold

Container-Grown trees are sold in pots filled with soil and have established root systems, which makes them easier to transplant. They are usually more expensive because the plants have been nurtured.

Balled-and-Burlapped young trees are sold with their roots surrounded in balls of soil wrapped in burlap. Even large evergreens such as spruce and pine are often sold in this manner. It is essential that the root ball be consistently moist. Ball-and-burlapped trees are sometimes displayed at garden centers in large wooden boxes filled with wood chips. Such trees are often too heavy to lift, and may require the additional expenses of delivery and mechanical planting.

Bare-Root trees are sold with their roots not covered by soil or container. It is important that the roots be kept consistently moist and

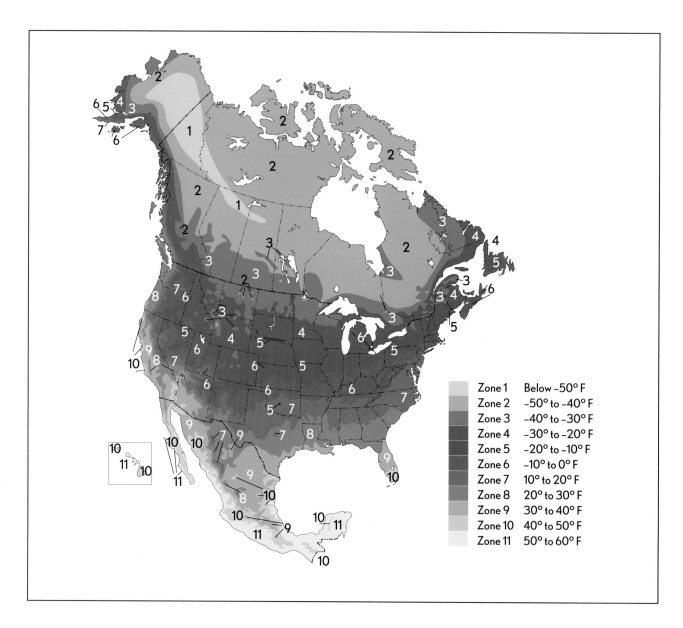

Zone 1	Below −50° F
Zone 2	−50° to −40° F
Zone 3	−40° to −30° F
Zone 4	−30° to −20° F
Zone 5	−20° to −10° F
Zone 6	−10° to 0° F
Zone 7	10° to 20° F
Zone 8	20° to 30° F
Zone 9	30° to 40° F
Zone 10	40° to 50° F
Zone 11	50° to 60° F

Range of average annual minimum temperature for each zone.

cool prior to planting. Bare-root trees must not be subjected to freezing temperatures during shipping. These trees are less expensive than container-grown plants and those that are balled-and-burlapped.

Other Tips to Consider When Purchasing a Tree

Look for your specimen early in the season, before the tree's roots suffer from root bound, because they've been growing in pots all season long.

Signs of root damage include drooping and/or browned **candles** (lighter-colored and softer new growth at the ends of branches) and dry needles with pines and spruces that fall off. If your new tree turns brown shortly after planting, its roots may have been injured before you purchased it. Check with your nursery about its guarantee policy before purchasing a tree.

Trained evergreens, such as juniper or weeping Norway Spruce, or

TREES THAT ARE SUITABLE FOR SANDY SOIL:

Norway Maple
Silver Maple
Hackberry
Linden
Honey Locust
Catalpa
Red Pine
Jack Pine
Colorado Spruce
Siberian Elm
Staghorn Sumac

TREES THAT ARE SUITABLE FOR WET SOIL:

Red Maple
Willow
White Oak
Pin Oak
Cedar
Larch
Basswood
Silver Maple
European Ash
Poplar
River Birch
Holly

TREES WITH INTERESTING BARK:

White Birch
London Plane Tree
Paperbark Maple
Scotch Pine
Blue Beech

American Beech
River Birch
Hop Tree

FLOWERING TREES:

Magnolia
Crab Apple
Eastern Redbud
Flowering Dogwood
Ornamental Pear
Serviceberry
Japanese Tree Lilac
Witch Hazel
Hawthorn
Japanese Flowering Cherry
Golden Chain Tree
Red Buckeye

SHADE OR LARGE TREES:

Tulip Tree
Oak (Red, White, Burr, etc.)
White Pine
Ginkgo
Little-leaf Linden
Dawn Redwood (deciduous evergreen)
Sugar Maple
Kentucky Coffee Tree
Katsuratree
Red Maple
Black Walnut
Black Locust
Sassafrass
Sweet Gum
Tamarak
Cucumber Tree

Lois Hole, author and gardener, suggests the following tips to increase your chances of success when experimenting in your own garden with out-of-zone plants:

- Only plant species that are naturally adapted to the type of soil in the new habitat.
- Evaluate exposure when planting a new tree, and choose an area of the garden that is sheltered from strong winds.
- Consider mulching the plant in late fall, and for at least the first winter.
- Water the plant well into late fall, shortly before the ground freezes.

grafted trees are sold staked; otherwise, these trees would grow flat along the ground. Some young trees are also sold staked so that their trunks stay straight, but don't buy larger trees with scrawny trunks that are staked.

1. The term **field-grown** indicates the tree was raised on a tree farm in a field where it was well watered with adequate room to grow.

If possible, choose field-grown when buying a balled-and-burlapped tree.

2. **Nursery-grown** trees tend to be thicker, more compact, and have stronger, more vigorous root systems than trees dug out of the wild.

Hardiness Rating

The accepted standard of determining the hardiness of a particular plant is called a zone rating. Zone maps are based chiefly on the minimum winter temperatures, but also take into account other issues such as the length of the growing season, soil conditions, and fluctuating temperatures. Canadian plant hardiness zones run from the coldest zone of 0 to the warmest zone of 9. The higher the zone, the greater number of plant species can be grown. By and large, the Canadian and US zone systems are interchangeable.

Because zone ratings may not accurately reflect the precise conditions in your garden, they should be used as a general guide rather than a hard-fast rule. To help determine the zone in your area, call a local garden center or talk to experienced gardeners. Remember that an out-of-zone tree will likely grow slowly, and may never attain its potential size.

A native tree naturally suited to the conditions of your site will grow easily, but it will face enormous stress if it is introduced to an environment where the conditions are very different from its native habitat. Some trees are more tolerable than others, but all trees react to rainfall, humidity, and temperature conditions. For example, a tree native to zone 6 may survive in warmer regions of zone 5 until low temperatures cause fatal freezing damage, whereas trees native to zone 5 will likely be able to withstand colder conditions.

Important factors to consider when selecting a tree

In order to choose the right tree you have to know what you want.

- What is the purpose or desired effect?
- What tree types are native to your area? What trees are available at your local garden center?
- What trees are best suited to your location?

Do you have the space for the tree? Picture the tree when it is mature or fully grown. Will it interfere with anything? A very common error is planting a tree too close to a building or to another tree. The tree may be small when planted, but as it matures it can crowd out other trees, resulting in both trees' struggling as they compete for space, light, and nutrients. Also, a tree planted too close to a building can cause a lot of problems. The tree may have to be severely pruned to clear branches from the structure, or removed completely because of interference with the building, or underground pipes may become blocked by roots. The key to avoiding these situations is to know how

When purchasing a tree for your garden, consider the many characteristics that trees offer, such as interesting bark, shape and size, fruit seeds, flowers and cones, leaf and needle formation, shade, and color.

big the tree you buy will get when it reaches maturity. Ideally, you should plant a tree that can reach its natural size in a spot where it is going to have lots of room to grow and not interfere with anything around it. Allow sufficient space to accommodate mature size. If the space is not sufficient, choose a smaller tree.

Is the tree hardy enough for your area? Know your hardiness zone. Trees and shrubs will be healthiest and look most attractive when provided with their preferred growing conditions.

Consider the drainage of the planting location, which is a very important but often overlooked factor in choosing a tree. Does the water drain well or does it pool and sit on top of the ground, leaving the area wet? Trees planted in a site that is too wet or too dry will often die in the first year.

Consider the soil type in your area. Certain trees are better suited to various soil conditions. Drainage is poor in a heavy clay soil, and a soil that is too sandy will be lacking in nutrients. Also, if the soil is compacted the growth of the tree will be reduced because of lack of oxygen in the root zone.

Tree characteristics

There are many characteristics to consider when choosing a tree for your space.

- Interesting bark.
- Different types of fruit seeds, flowers, and cones.
- Comfortable shade, either to relax under or to help moderate the temperature of your home, keeping it cool in summer.
- Sizes and shape. Columnar trees, for example grow very narrow and upright. Many trees have sculptural forms and shapes visible in the winter that offer interest during the long cold season.
- Inspiring color. Consider a blue spruce, with its beautiful blue color, or a crimson king maple, with its dark purple leaves.
- The color and shape of the leaves. The tulip tree has a delightful leaf, as does the mulberry, which can have two or three different-shaped leaves on the same branch. The compound leaves of the Kentucky coffee tree or the black walnut are pleasing. Ginkjo leaves are fan shaped.
- Appeal to wildlife. Coniferous trees, for example, provide excellent shelter for wildlife.
- Delicious fruit, such as pears, cherries, apples, etc.
- Flowers, from the stunning saucer magnolia to the small yellow flower of the witch hazel, which that can last well into the winter.
- Some deciduous trees' leaves change and die, and can remain on the tree well into the winter season. Examples are the pyramidal English oak and the pin oak.
- Branching patterns, such as the zig-zag growth of the honey locust tree or the upright spreading growth of the zelkova tree.

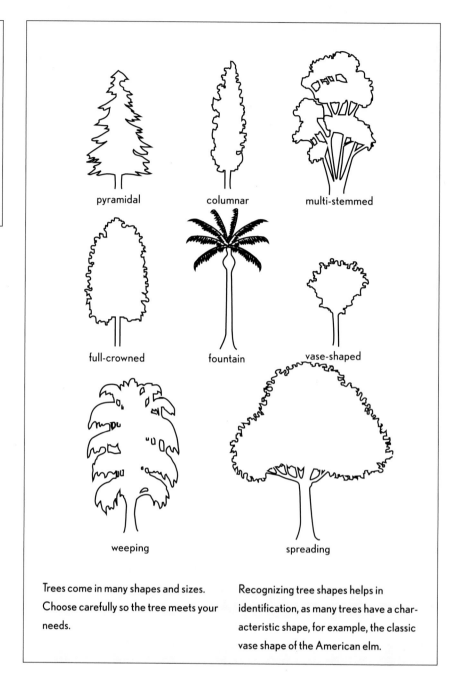

pyramidal   columnar   multi-stemmed

full-crowned   fountain   vase-shaped

weeping   spreading

Trees come in many shapes and sizes. Choose carefully so the tree meets your needs.

Recognizing tree shapes helps in identification, as many trees have a characteristic shape, for example, the classic vase shape of the American elm.

Refer to page 31 for a few examples of tree types with specific characteristics, to help you consider the options available. Bear in mind that there are literally hundreds of species to choose from so consult the many informative gardening magazines and books that feature trees in different regions. It is worth reviewing publications with comprehensive lists and details, such as *The Encyclopedia of Trees: Canada and the United States, Lois Hole's Favorite Trees & Shrubs, Ortho's All About Trees*, and *Sunset Trees & Shrubs*.

Decide what characteristics you find attractive and what purpose you have in mind when choosing a tree. Take a walk around your neighborhood and see what kinds of trees have been planted and

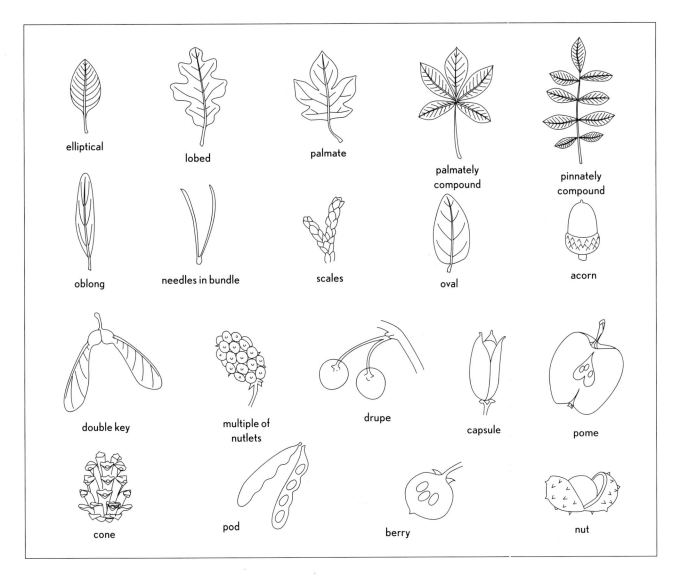

elliptical

lobed

palmate

palmately
compound

pinnately
compound

oblong

needles in bundle

scales

oval

acorn

double key

multiple of
nutlets

drupe

capsule

pome

cone

pod

berry

nut

how they are used. Visit a tree nursery, look at the selection of trees, and ask questions of the nursery staff.

You may be inspired by what you see planted in neighboring properties and decide to buy a certain tree, but not know what kind of tree it is. One option is to ask the owner if you may take a small twig sample using your gardening secateurs. Then take it to your local nursery or garden center. Knowledgeable staff should be able to inform you of its species type. However, you can also identify trees yourself with the help of a good reference book. Leaves are often the most identifiable features on a tree, but in the winter you will have to examine other parts instead. Look at the tree's overall structure, the type of bark and buds, and seeds or fruit on the tree. Most plant reference books have a series of keys that you can follow to determine tree species. Just follow the keys, using all the features you observed.

Leaf shapes and sizes provide interest in the landscape. Fruits and cones can attract wildlife, offer variety and can remain on branches in the winter, providing winter enjoyment. Leaves, fruits, and cones are all identification features.

ABOVE TOP: Trees create privacy for urban dwellers.

ABOVE: Trees make excellent natural fences or screens.

Planning and design

Take a careful look at your space and think about the following points when you are selecting trees and considering where to place them:

- Purpose. Do you want to feature trees in your garden for privacy? Do you want a tree that will produce flowers for cutting? Do you want a companion piece to the architecture of your house? A natural element in crowded urban area? A property line or barrier? A specimen or accent plant?
- Theme. Is there a particular type of garden you want to create, such as a lush Victorian setting or a spare modern landscape?
- Maintenance. How much time do you have to tend to your trees?
- Continuity. Do your plans complement the area surrounding your garden space?
- Seriously consider where you are going to plant, because transplanting trees and shrubs causes stress.
- As a general rule, install plants from largest to smallest (placing the smallest at the front).
- Root competition and shade. You must acknowledge a tree's natural dominance when choosing other plants to grow around it.
- Cost!
- Envision the tree's appearance in all seasons.
- Consider the plant's susceptibility to pests or disease. For example, the European white birch is a poor choice if you live east of the Rockies (where bronze birch borer zeroes in), but a good choice for the western states (where the pest is absent).
- Windbreaks reduce wind, noise, and soil erosion, and they help to retain moisture by collecting snow and by creating a milder microclimate for nearby plants. Study where windbreaks should be planted to ensure greatest amount of protection for plants and buildings.

Review these special concerns for particular sites:

- Watch out for overhead or underground utility lines, septic tanks, or other physical constraints.
- Call city hall and/or the electric company about curbside or street trees, as they may have lists of trees that are recommended or not permitted. The ideal street trees are short, neat, care-free and tough, with strong limbs that don't fall off.
- Consider planting small, slender trees with fragrant flowers, berries that attract birds, fancy foliage, or interesting bark next to a patio or deck.
- The lawn is the best place for a large tree if you have the space. Make sure the tree has an open canopy that doesn't cast too much shade, has roots that never appear at the surface, and will adapt to

Bear in mind the amount of litter certain trees can create. Flowers and fruit will fall from trees and need to be cleaned up. Fruit will rot if left on the ground, and attract insects such as bees or wasps. Fast-growing trees such as the willow or poplar tend to have weak wood and can drop small twigs and branches, especially during windy conditions. Some years trees will produce an abundance of seeds, and cones from evergreen trees can cause quite a mess.

Walk around your neighborhood and see what kinds of trees appear to be thriving. If you have difficulty identifying a tree, ask the owner's permission then take a small twig or leaf sample to your local garden center, or refer to a tree reference book with keys you can follow to determine tree species.

As you begin to familiarize yourself with a wide variety of trees, take note of how a tree looks during different seasons. Pick out certain features that will help you recognize the tree throughout the year, without leaves for example. Observe the shape, structure, bark, fruit, and flowers as they present themselves at different times of the year. One good identifying feature to know is the tree's buds. You will realize that buds can be very distinctive; you won't forget the large sticky bud of the horse chestnut tree or the long pointed cigar-shaped buds of the beech tree. Upon closer examination, you will notice that tree buds are usually opposite or alternately placed on the twig. Knowing if the buds are opposite or alternate will narrow your list of possibilities. Get to know your buds, using a good tree ID book, and enjoy discovering the wide variety of trees in the landscape.

the same watering and fertilizing practices that you use for the lawn.
- You need height and density for a screening effect, not width, so look for narrow, upright varieties. Tall, skinny trees that keep their lower limbs are uncommon, but can be special-ordered from a local garden center.

Planting for landscape enhancement and functionality

- Within every yard there are **microclimates**, areas that may be either warmer or colder than surrounding areas. On a fall morning after a freezing night, you will sometimes notice that frost has hit only certain exposed spots in your yard. Trees help produce microclimates. The warmest parts of your garden will be near tall trees or large shrubs, hedges, fences, and walls. Such obstructions trap heat and provide shelter from the wind. Select protected spots for tender plant varieties and reserve exposed areas for hardier plants.
- Newly planted evergreens and non-hardy specimens should be planted in locations that stress them least—ideally, sites that are sunny in summer and shaded during winter.
- Tender evergreens such as rhododendrons are most susceptible to foliage damage.
- Rather than choosing a tree that will grow too large for its site, pick a named cultivar of the chosen species with a small growth habit, or dwarf or weeping characteristics.
- By choosing a variety of trees, you add diversity to the area, which

Opt for a cultivar or dwarf species if you have limited space for a tree.

strengthens the ecology of the region, nurturing wildlife and promoting healthy plants that are more tolerant of disease, pests, and drought.

- ➤ Deciduous versus evergreen. Most deciduous trees start their growth in spring, with a burst of new leaves or flowers, and last the summer in full foliage. Leaf color often changes in the fall before the leaves drop. Winter can reveal a fascinating structure of bare limbs. Broad-leafed evergreens are not generally able to survive in extremely cold winter climates. Needle-leafed evergreens include those with actual needles—pine, fir, and

If you're lucky enough to own a large property, check with your local conservation authority or government agencies to see if they provide tree seedlings or whips to plant on your property. There may also be incentives for planting trees on your property. You will benefit your area and the environment by planting trees in large quantities.

Trees can be grown for lumber, fine wood for furniture, and other purposes. Black walnut is particularly valued for its wood for furniture. Cherry wood is sought for fine furniture. Mature trees of these species can be worth a lot of money. Sugar maples can be grown and tapped for their sap, which is made into maple syrup.

spruce—as well as junipers and cypresses, whose leaves are merely tiny scales. All evergreens keep their uniform appearance all year long, though they lose some foliage every year.

- Strive for harmony and scale within your garden to create enduring beauty. Your trees will be celebrated for generations to come.

What makes a tree suitable for the city?

Urban communities are beautifully suited to tree plantings, because trees help to decrease air and noise pollution and can make our city streets look more natural. However, city life creates challenges for

Urban gardeners should select a specimen that won't outgrow its space. Decorative small-sized trees include eastern redbud, pagoda dogwood, Japanese tree lilac, serviceberry, or paperbark maple.

homeowners, so consider the following points when selecting a tree for your space:

- Select a hardy tree that is able to tolerate road salt used in winter, and air pollution such as emissions from cars and trucks.
- Choose a tree resistant to insect and disease problems to avoid the use of chemical pesticides.
- If the tree can tolerate drought conditions, it can survive in harsh urban conditions.
- Crab apple and mountain ash trees provide beautiful flowers in the spring. But weak-wooded trees such as willows, poplars, and silver maple can drop small twigs or branches, and flowering trees will drop their petals. Can you tolerate such messes?
- A tree that provides shade may be highly prized; nevertheless, heavy shade will result in a poor lawn.

Common complaints about street trees:

- Messiness (crab apple, mountain ash).
- Too much foliage/shade: grass does not grow, sap or waste from insects drips on cars or driveways, causing damage (Norway maple).
- Roots from trees heave or crack driveway, walkway, or foundation (silver maple).
- Branches obstruct view of traffic on road when backing out of driveway (spruce, cedar, juniper).
- Street trees interfere with residents' private trees, and impede their growth.
- Street trees block or restrict light from a streetlight.

How you can maintain your street tree

Municipalities throughout North America encourage residents to plant trees to help decrease pollution. In addition, many local governments plant trees along city streets and employ **arborists** and forestry workers to maintain them. Often, homeowners can even choose the type of tree they would like featured on their street. If you have a city tree on your lot, consider the following tips to help maintain its health:

- Avoid damaging the trunk with weed eaters and lawn mowers. Damage to the bark can kill the tree.
- Do not mound soil or grass clippings around the trunk of the tree.
- If you maintain a healthy lawn and boulevard, a mature tree will usually receive sufficient water. However, it is advisable to supply water to the tree in excessively dry periods. Also, newly planted trees need plenty of water. Because it is difficult for municipali-

Maintain your city street tree by avoiding damage inflicted by weed eaters and lawn mowers, and then by watering when necessary.

ties to water these trees on a regular basis, you may want to take on this job.

- Contact your municipality to have the tree pruned to remove low, interfering limbs. General pruning will also benefit the overall health of the tree.
- Avoid planting flowers under the tree or piling rocks against the trunk of the tree.
- A wood chip mulch of 3 to 4 inches around the base of the tree (but not against the trunk) will help retain moisture, moderate soil temperature, and reduce weed growth.

Chapter 3

PLANTING AND CARE AFTER PLANTING

PLANTING

Careful attention to tree placement and planting can ensure a life-time of enjoyment. Successful planting requires choosing a healthy specimen and then carefully planting it at the time of year most suitable for good root growth.

Plant death is frequently caused by improper planting and inadequate follow-up care. A close look at planting techniques will ensure your trees get off to a good start and will help you achieve long-term success in establishing your home landscape.

Soil basics

You need to know the character of your soil before you can prepare it for planting. Soil is a complex environment, containing not only mineral particles but also organic matter, air, water, and organisms from earthworms to microscopic bacteria. For good growth, plants need water, air, and nutrients.

The sizes and shapes of mineral particles account for physical characteristics of "heavy" or "light" soil extremes. Clay particles are tiny and flattened, fitting closely together. Soils comprising mainly clay particles have little space between particles so water percolates through slowly. Clay soil retains dissolved nutrients, but because drainage is slow, clay soil can be deficient in soil air if overwatered. Clay soil is also slow to warm up in spring. Clay soil feels slick to the touch.

Sandy soil has particles that are much larger and irregularly rounded, resulting in a gritty feel. These soils fit together more loosely, leaving relatively large spaces between particles. Water percolates easily. Sandy soil is well drained and well aerated, but needs frequent water and nutrient applications to maintain adequate moisture and fertility.

Amending soil, although practiced by some, is not recommended at the time of planting unless the soil is builder's waste or pure sand. Fill your hole with the removed soil, not peat moss, compost, or bagged soil. It is best to get the tree immediately accustomed to the soil in which it will be growing. Otherwise, the roots tend to stay in the amended soil and never grow into the surrounding native soil.

Mulch is a beneficial and aesthetically pleasing ground cover.

Fall versus spring planting:

- Experienced gardeners know that fall is an ideal time to plant new trees. In the fall, it is easy to see where the tree fits in because of the lack of full foliage. Cool weather is less stressful to trees than hot, dry summer. Shrubs, trees, and evergreens will be noticeably advanced with regard to growth and bloom compared with those planted next spring. The younger feeder roots of trees planted in the fall provide the necessary water and nutrients for the plant to become established, resulting in substantial new growth as soon as the soil begins to warm at the start of a new planting season.

- Spring is a peak time for selection and choice. It is the best time to plant trees that are not locally grown, to allow them to adjust to new climate conditions. Trees still have plenty of time to set their roots before the stress of summer heat.

The best soils contain a mixture of particle sizes and shapes, balancing clay's nutrient-holding capacity with sand's permeability. Fortunately, most soils fall somewhere between the extremes of clay and sand, and need little special treatment to grow trees and shrubs well.

Nevertheless, these following soil conditions usually require special treatment:

- Compact soil—In new housing developments, the soil will have been compressed by heavy equipment during construction. Such soil is poorly drained, difficult to dig, and nearly impossible for roots to penetrate. Special soil-loosening equipment may remedy the situation; contact an arborist. The alternative is to construct raised beds and fill them with good soil.
- Shallow soil—A shallow layer of good soil may be found on new home sites where the developer has spread new soil over the soil compacted during construction. Shallow soil may also occur naturally, over a layer of dense hardpan; in the Southwest, gardeners must cope with an alkaline hardpan known as **caliche**. If a hardpan layer is thin, you may be able to dig full-width planting holes through it to more porous soil beneath. You could consider planting a little higher, like you would for a clay soil—add soil and mulch to the top of the root ball (but don't bury it).
- Acid or alkaline soil—You may be able to moderate chemical extremes with soil treatments available from nurseries, but you'll need to repeat treatment, depending on the result you require. Amending soil to optimum conditions is difficult to achieve, and such a result is not permanent. You'll have to apply treatment regularly.

A far simpler approach than amending soil is to choose trees that will thrive in the normal acidity or alkalinity of your soil. Your soil is one of three types: acid, alkaline, or neutral.

This characteristic is measured in pH, with a pH of 7 representing neutral. Readings of less than 7 indicate **acid** soil, higher than 7, **alkaline**. If readings are extreme in either direction, key nutrients are bound up tightly in compounds in the soil and not available to roots. Most trees and shrubs will prosper in soils registering a pH of 5.5 to 6.5. A soil test will confirm your pH. Soil test kits sold at nurseries will give you ballpark readings, but professional tests will provide more precise results.

When to plant

The best time of year to plant depends on your climate and the type of tree you are planting. In general, planting should be done in the spring (March through May) and the fall (October through

November), because increased soil moisture and moderate temperatures are favorable conditions for planting. Aim to plant the tree early enough in the spring or fall to allow the roots to grow and establish before the harsher conditions of summer or winter arrive. Certain trees are better planted in the spring so they have more time to get established. Consult local nursery staff about the appropriate time to plant a specific tree.

In the southern US, planting can also take place during the winter months. Summer planting is never recommended, because heat and drought are especially stressful to newly planted trees. In milder regions, where the soil seldom freezes, you can plant trees and shrubs throughout the year, though fall through winter is the preferred period. In colder regions, late winter to early spring will get most plants off to the best start.

Some gardeners prefer to plant trees in the fall, after dormancy sets in but at least a month before the soil freezes. Cooler weather allows for more comfort while digging, while trees and shrubs still have time to put their roots into the soil before temperatures drop. The young feeder roots of trees planted in the fall provide the necessary water and nutrients for plants to become established, resulting in substantial new growth as soon as the soil begins to warm through at the start of spring. Trees planted the previous fall will grow and bloom more quickly than trees newly planted in spring.

When spring planting, ensure maximum first-year growth with the least stress on a new plant by planting in advance of the growing season, while the soil is cool. This will give roots a chance to grow into the new soil before foliage growth begins, which places demands on the root system.

- Balled-and-burlapped trees are available to be planted from early autumn and springtime. Remember, the root ball must not be allowed to dry out.
- Bare-root trees are available only during autumn and winter, when they are dormant. Their roots, which must be kept moist before planting, are buried in a moisture-retentive medium.
- Container-grown trees are available whenever the ground is not frozen. They are best planted in cooler months, but may be set during spring or summer if you water adequately during dry periods and shelter the tree from intense sun and wind.

How to dig a planting hole

- Call your local utility company before you dig to check for underground wires.
- When digging in poorly drained clay soil, avoid glazing, which occurs when the sides and bottom of the hole become smooth, forming a barrier through which water and roots may not pass.

Use your shovel to gauge the depth of your hole. Place the shovel in the hole and check the level of the desired planting depth with your finger on the handle of the shovel, and match that to the tree's root ball to get approximate depth of hole.

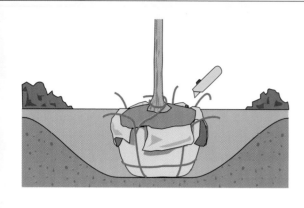

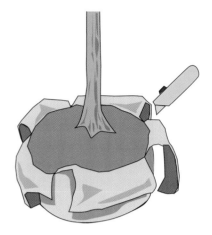

When the tree has been set in the hole at the proper depth and straightened, before backfilling, be sure to cut rope from around the trunk and ball. Either peel back burlap below ground level or cut back so none of the burlap is above the soil. If the ball is in a wire basket, cut back the top one-third of the basket.

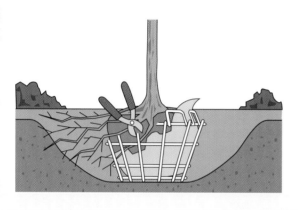

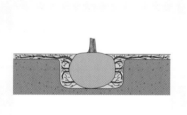

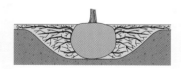

A properly dug planting hole provides roots with optimal growing conditions. A broad planting hole (bottom), two to three times the size of the root ball, is ideal.

Glazing will inhibit proper root development into the surrounding soil. Use a fork to rough up the sides and bottom of the hole.

- The width of the hole should be two to three times the size of the root ball of the tree you are planting.
- The hole should be saucer-shaped, so the roots can spread horizontally near the surface, where optimum growth takes place.
- Planting depth is important. A common mistake is to plant too deep. If you plant too deeply the roots won't have access to sufficient oxygen to ensure proper growth; if you dig too narrow the root structure won't expand to nourish and anchor the tree. The tree should not look like a telephone pole going into the ground, i.e., the trunk should have a flare to it and be wider at the bottom, tapering as it extends upwards.
- Dig more deeply around the edges of the hole's bottom. This leaves a slight mound of undug soil to support the plant at a proper depth and prevents settling of the tree and pooling of water.
- It is best to have the root collar 1 to 3 inches higher than ground level because of possible settling. If possible, try to orient the tree in the same direction it was grown—ask the staff at a tree farm in which direction it grew. Position it for best viewing, and face the lowest branches away from the greatest pedestrian and vehicular traffic.

The preceding section addresses how to dig a basic planting hole for all kinds of trees—the steps below address how to plant specific tree stock.

How to plant

Balled-and-Burlapped

- The burlap should not be removed until your tree is positioned in the hole and straight, in order to keep the roots intact.
- Set your balled-and-burlapped tree in the planting hole, with its root ball resting on the mound of undug soil.
- Untie the burlap and spread it out, uncovering half of the root ball. Gently cut away loose burlap without damaging the root ball and cut any rope away from the trunk.
- If there is a wire basket around the root ball, cut it so it will not impede growth of the trunk. Then trim away the top one-third of the wire basket. Be sure no sharp pieces of the basket protrude through the soil.
- Leave the remaining burlap and/or wire under the root ball— roots grow out, not down.
- When the tree is positioned and straight, **backfill** the hole to just below the root collar, using the same soil that you dug out. Break up any large clumps and remove any debris. Amending the soil is not recommended, as roots tend to stay in pockets of amended soil instead of reaching out to become established. Lightly pack the backfill around the root ball. Once the hole is half full, pour a bit of water over the tree roots to help eliminate any air pockets that may be present. Continue to backfill, tamping. (Do not pack the soil after you water.) Create a raised berm or dike around the root ball to help retain moisture around the roots.

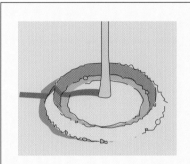

Forming a berm or dike around the outer edge of the root ball will help collect water, keeping the root area moist.

These key steps in planting are quick and easy, but it is surprising how often they are forgotten. Many trees' root balls are girdled when rope is not removed from the trunk. This will kill the tree, as water and nutrient uptake is impossible. Also, burlap left exposed aboveground acts like a wick to dry out the root ball, killing roots that are vital for plant establishment. Be careful not to pile dirt against the tree trunk—this can cause bark rot.

Balled-and-burlapped trees are best planted as soon as possible after delivery, but they can be stored for a few weeks in a shady area as long as the root ball is moist. Balled-and-burlapped trees are generally larger than containerized trees and can weigh hundreds of pounds.

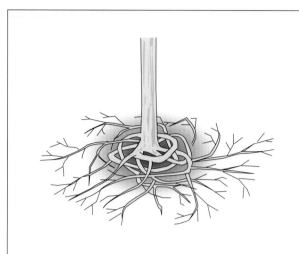

Trees grown in containers, or bare-root trees that have been potted, can have circling roots that can girdle other roots or the trunk. Circling roots should be separated and spread out when planting.

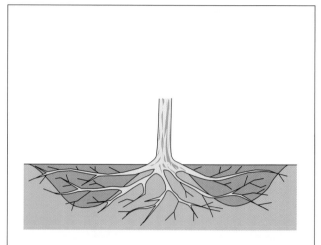

Bare-root trees should be planted on a compacted soil mound. Spread the roots out over the mound, keeping them from crossing and becoming tangled.

Bare-root

1. Build a cone of earth in the center of the hole, around which to spread the roots. Spread roots over the cone, placing your plant at the same depth (or a bit higher) as it was in the growing field.
2. Add backfill soil nearly to the top of the hole, tamping it as you fill. Add water. If the plant settles, move it up and down in the saturated soil to raise it to the proper level.

Plant bare-root trees during the dormant season, before roots and buds begin to grow. Plant as soon as possible after delivery, but if you cannot plant immediately, store the tree in a cool area with moist packing around the roots until you're ready to plant it, the sooner the better.

Container plants

1. The roots of container plants may be coiled or matted. Remove the container and remove the soil from the outer few inches of the root ball, then uncoil circling or twisted roots with your fingers or a blunt instrument.
2. Lightly break up soil around the sides of the planting zone to allow roots that spread quickly to easily extend and grow outward as they anchor into existing soil conditions.
3. Spread the roots out over the mound of soil in the center of the hole. The top of the root ball should be approximately 2 inches above surrounding soil.
4. Add backfill soil.

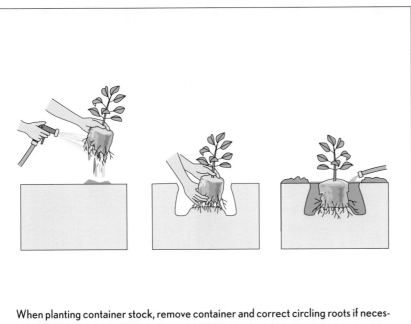

When planting container stock, remove container and correct circling roots if necessary. Spray the outer few inches of the root ball with water to aid in correcting circling roots. Spread roots over compacted mound and backfill. Create a berm to water.

Containerized trees are usually sold in plastic or natural fiber pots. Although easy to handle and plant, their roots can become potbound or circling, which can inhibit root growth. Roots can also become girdled or be choked out by other circling roots. Be sure to check the root structure before purchasing a containerized tree. A container plant can be stored for a brief period in a shady area as long as the soil in the container is kept moist.

Before planting, slide the tree out of the container and gently score the sides with a knife to encourage rooting. Trees that come in natural fiber pots can be left in pots when planted, but you should cut the top portion of pots away to ensure that no part of a pot is exposed above soil level. Remove metal or plastic containers completely.

Planting trees in aboveground containers

Trees planted in aboveground containers have a difficult time surviving and are unlikely to live very long. There are a number of reasons:

- Containers hold only small amounts of soil.
- Roots cannot tolerate extreme changes in temperature. Soil temperature is relatively stable belowground. Tree roots in aboveground containers can bake in the summer and freeze in the winter. However, insulated containers are better able to withstand extreme temperatures than non-insulated ones.
- Soil in aboveground containers can dry out quickly, so these plants must be watered regularly. They cannot survive on rainfall alone.

To help increase the life of your tree planted in an aboveground container, make sure the container is insulated and that there is adequate drainage.

• Often, containers do not provide adequate drainage, which means that roots can become waterlogged and the trees can drown. Make sure your containers have drainage holes.

If you want to plant in aboveground containers, choose small trees with small root systems. You may need to replace aboveground trees every two to five years.

Help ensure that your trees enjoy a long life by completing the following maintenance tasks.

- Staking only when necessary. Most newly planted trees will be fine if they are not staked. But if your tree is placed in an open, windy area, staking provides a young tree with support until the root system is established in the new location.
- Mulching. Use only organic mulch such as wood chips or bark chips.
- Watering. Watering is imperative in order for roots to grow into surrounding soil. To test if your tree needs water, feel the soil 4 to 8 inches deep—if it's dry or only slightly damp, add water. Sandy soil will require more water than the clay soil, which tends to hold moisture longer. Water the tree surrounding the trunk. A slow trickle from the garden hose left to run over several hours is more beneficial than short, frequent watering, which promotes a shallow root system and makes the tree more vulnerable to environmental stress. Continue until mid fall, tapering off for lower temperatures that require less frequent watering. Give each of your trees one good long soak before freeze-up. Pay particular attention to evergreens, which lose moisture all winter because they don't shed their needles.
- Fertilizing. Fertilizing may be necessary if your soil is deficient in essential macro and micro nutrients.

Watering long and deep will benefit the growth and health of your tree.

CARE AFTER PLANTING

Since trees are such a visible part of the landscape, care must be taken to ensure that proper growth conditions are maintained. Trees lose 70 to 95 percent of their root mass when transplanted, and it usually takes transplanted trees one year for every inch of trunk diameter to regenerate root mass.

Pruning at the time of planting is not recommended, and should be limited to dead wood, broken branches, and damaged limbs. Corrective pruning activity—such as pruning interfering limbs, poorly spaced limbs, and weak crotches—should wait until the tree is established, after one or two growing seasons.

Watering

Proper watering practices are vital to the survival of your newly planted tree. Trees need soil moisture to encourage root growth and to supply water to leaves. Watering practices should suit the plant type and its environment, and must be appropriate for soil type and drainage. Young plants getting established need more attention, as do mature specimens with extensive root systems.

Your soil type will also influence your watering schedule. Clay needs less frequent, but deeper, watering for the water to penetrate.

Every newly planted tree should be well watered at planting to eliminate air pockets and settle the tree firmly in place. Moisture should reach 12 inches below the soil surface to encourage ideal

If you decide your young tree should be staked, stake it only for a year or so. Although you'll often see trees staked with wire and rubber, as illustrated, this is not recommended. You should use a biodegradable material such as burlap instead.

growth. Thereafter, water once or twice a week for the first few weeks until the root system becomes established. (Be careful not to overwater. Surprisingly, overwatering kills more trees than underwatering. Too much will cause leaves to turn yellow or fall off.)

Check the soil to determine when you need to water. For newly planted trees, water thoroughly when the top inch of soil has dried. For established trees, you may be able to wait until the top 2 to 4 inches of soil have lost moisture. You seldom need to water mature trees, except during periods of drought.

Prolonged rainfall will supply enough water to penetrate deeply. If you use sprinklers to duplicate rainfall, allow water to soak into soil over a period of time, which will provide the best penetration with the least waste through runoff and evaporation. You can use a soaker hose too—called "drip irrigation."

Continue watering until mid-fall, tapering off as temperatures lower. In cold-winter regions, water trees well in advance of hard freezes. Give each of your trees one good, long soaking before freeze-up. Plants that enter winter in dry soil have no moisture reserves in their needles to thwart drying winter winds. Evergreen plants are especially vulnerable to dry soil.

Staking

Staking is often used to reestablish young trees, especially bare-root stock. Some argue that staking is not necessary, and that trees will develop better if they are not staked. However, you might consider staking if your tree is planted in a very windy or exposed location.

Transplanted trees suffer root loss, and root loss limits a tree's ability to take in water and nutrients. Once a tree is planted, it will concentrate its energy on standing upright. To keep it straight and to keep it from being blown over, a young transplanted tree may be staked for a year or so.

Proper staking will also allow your tree enough room to move with the wind, which will enable the tree to develop a good trunk taper, which is important for stability. Staking will help to reduce movement of the root ball, which may cause damage to new fine absorbing roots.

For best anchorage and to prevent damage, at least two stakes should be used for each tree and installed with the following tips in mind:

- Set stakes at equal distances from the trunk.
- Drive stakes into solid undisturbed ground at least 2 feet deep from the trunk to provide adequate stability for the tree and to avoid the root ball.
- Tie the tree to the stakes with suitable biodegradable material such as burlap. Avoid using wire encased in rubber hose as this will not allow trunk expansion if left on too long.
- Leave at least 1 inch of space between each tie and the tree trunk. Remove stakes and ties after 1 year. If it is too dependent on supports, the trunk will not develop adequate strength.

If you decide to stake your tree, remember:

- Stake only the tree until it is able to stand on its own. If it is too dependent on supports, the trunk will not develop adequate strength.
- The staking material should not be too tight. Leave room for the tree to sway in the wind.
- The material should not be too loose. The tree should not rub against its stakes.
- Stakes should be buried to at least 2 feet to provide ample support.
- Place your stakes carefully, so people won't trip over them.

Trunk protection

You may choose to use a plastic tree guard around the trunk to minimize damage caused by mice, rabbits, and other animals, as well as mowers and string trimmers. (Wrapping, another procedure

A plastic tree guard offers young trees protection from trunk and bark damage caused by mice and rabbits and mechanical injury.

sometimes used on young trees where a material such as burlap and crepe paper is wrapped around bark, is not recommended, because it fosters an environment for boring insects.) The guard should be loose fitting and allow air to circulate around the trunk. Protect young trees against winter chewing of the bark by mice, rabbits or deer with plastic spirals.

Fertilizing

Trees growing in the wild get no fertilizer as we think of it. But annual layers of fallen leaves and animal droppings decompose to release a small but continuous supply of nutrients. In the same way, many trees may grow successfully in yards and gardens with no supplemental nutrients. If your tree displays strong new growth with good color each year, it is healthy and strong.

However, urban trees likely are growing in soils that do not contain sufficient available elements for satisfactory growth. As trees and shrubs grow and develop, they require nutrients such as nitrogen, phosphorous, and potassium. Topsoil is often removed during construction, and leaves and other plant parts are removed in gardening maintenance, thereby robbing the soil of nutrients and organic matter. Consequently, most woody plants in urban areas benefit from the addition of fertilizer.

Fertilizing is not necessary if your tree appears to be healthy and strong, but in some cases, for example when your soil does not contain sufficient nutrients, fertilizing would be beneficial.

Nitrogen, phosphorous and potassium are available to plants in different ways:

- Phosphorous and potassium must be present in the soil to be useful. Roots extract these two nutrients from films of water surrounding soil particles or from the particles themselves. The best time to apply fertilizer containing these two nutrients is before you plant, digging it well into the soil.
- Nitrogen is available to plants from the air, decaying matter in the soil, and fertilizer supplements. Much of the nitrogen in soil is lost due to leaching or to the return of nitrogen to the atmosphere in its gaseous state. Removing leaf litter and other natural sources of nitrogen can disrupt the cycling of nitrogen in the soil.

A fertilizer containing all three of the above nutrients is called a **complete fertilizer** (5-10-5 nitrogen-phosphorus-potassium). Fertilizers are available in organic or inorganic forms. Inorganic are quick releasing when dissolved in water, whereas organic fertilizers dissolve at a slower rate. Examples of natural organics are manures, sewage sludge, blood, and bone meal.

Use fertilizers with slow- or controlled-release nitrogen when fertilizing trees. To determine if it's a slow release, look for the percentage of water-insoluble nitrogen on the label. If approximately half of the nitrogen is water-insoluble, it is considered slow release.

In order for fertilizers to be absorbed by tree roots, the nutrients must be in solution, which requires soil moisture. So you must water thoroughly after applying fertilizer so the fertilizer is released.

Trees in a natural setting create their own mulch yearly, as they drop their leaves, twigs, fruit, flowers, etc. This litter layer provides many benefits for a tree. In an urban environment, you can mimic this by using an organic wood chip mulch around trees. When applied correctly, your tree will benefit greatly.

Mulching benefits:
- Reduces weed problems.
- Reduces soil compaction and erosion.
- Retains moisture.
- Moderates soil temperatures.
- Improves soil aeration and structure.
- Looks good.

Use composted mulch and apply at a depth of 2 to 4 inches, depending on the soil. For poorly drained soils such as clay, use 2 to 3 inches of mulch, and 3 to 4 inches for more well-drained soils. Spread the mulch wide, not deep. To avoid moist bark conditions and prevent decay, take care that the mulch doesn't touch the trunk of the tree.

Advantages of fertilizing

- Fertilizers address nutrient deficiencies. Plants lacking in nitrogen display slow growth, small leaves, and yellowing (chlorosis) of leaves. The application of fertilizer can often correct the problem.
- A tree that is growing vigorously is less susceptible to severe injury by certain disease and insect pests.

Disadvantages
Heavy nitrogen fertilization promotes vegetative growth, or green leaf growth, which may delay flowering output. High rates of application in July and August will stimulate growth, which won't harden off properly before the winter, and can result in winter kill. Heavy nitrogen fertilization can also stimulate the activity of sap-sucking insects and certain diseases.

Application

Surface application with dry fertilizer is an easy and effective way to fertilize trees. Spread the necessary quantity of fertilizer uniformly over the root zone and then water slowly but thoroughly. The zone of actively absorbing roots begins well beyond the drip line of the tree and is approximately one and one half to two times the crown radius.

To water and fertilize at the same time, apply fertilizer in a water suspension. The fertilizer solution is forced into the soil through a root feeder, a perforated, hollow rod attached to a source of water. Attach a hose to the root feeder, insert fertilizer pellets or cartridges into a chamber at the top of the unit, and then push the rod 12 inches into the soil, starting a few feet from the trunk and out beyond the drip line at 3-foot intervals. For best results, follow the manufacturer's instructions.

Timing

Trees particularly need nutrients when producing new growth. The best time to apply fertilizer is in late winter to early spring, depending on the climate. Fertilizer uptake in deciduous trees corresponds with the time of root growth, which, in general, starts before bud break and ends after leaf drop. Fall is also a good time to fertilize trees; many trees continue to grow roots in the fall after the shoots have stopped growing.

To prevent fertilizer runoff in the spring, avoid application if the ground is frozen. During drought periods, roots will not readily absorb fertilizers. There is also additional risk of damage from salts.

In mild-winter regions with no frost, you can continue a fertilizer program through the summer. In cold-winter climates, discontinue fertilizer application in early summer—the new growth stimulated by later applications will be at risk when temperatures plummet. However, trees *can* benefit from one final application applied just before the first frost is expected. The plants have already stopped producing new growth, but roots are still able to absorb nutrients and store them for spring's growth push.

Fertilizing shrubs

Fertilize shrub beds by broadcasting dry fertilizer over the soil surface and then watering thoroughly. Or scratch slow-release granular and coated fertilizers into the soil, following the manufacturer's instructions.

For broadleaf evergreen shrubs such as rhododendrons and azaleas, use a fertilizer specific for acid soil, since it usually contains minor elements in addition to nitrogen, phosphorus, and potassium. Phosphorus helps with bud formation on azaleas and rhododendrons, while too much nitrogen can reduce flower buds.

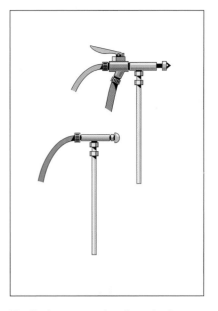

Used by homeowner, liquid root-feeding devices (left) are attached to a garden hose and have fertilizer cartridge chambers. Professional devices (right) use a spray tank under high pressure to deliver the fertilizer solution.

Mulch

In the wild, the forest floor is covered with a natural mulch made up of decomposing leaves, twigs, branches, and other plant and animal matter. Mulch keeps roots cool in summer and warm in winter. It keeps weeds down, helps retain moisture, improves soil structure, and reduces erosion and compaction. It also looks great. Studies have shown that wood chip mulch can nearly double a tree's growth rate during the first few years after planting. Mulch also fertilizes as it breaks down.

After planting, spread a 2- to 4-inch layer of mulch on the entire planting area, staying 3 inches from the tree trunk. Mulch mounded against a tree's trunk can cause crown rot and make the tree vulnerable to disease and insect problems. The broader the mulched area the better, but don't make it too deep. Spread the mulch in the shape of a saucer, not a mound, because a saucer shape will hold and distribute rainwater to a tree's roots. A "moat" of mulch will also protect an urban tree from damage caused by lawn mowers and weed cutters.

The most common tree mulch is wood chips. Available from a variety of sources, it often can be obtained at no charge through your local municipality (especially after Christmas trees are recycled!). The wood-chip mulch should be well composted, not fresh, because breaking down fresh wood can use up nitrogen required by the plant. Compost made of decomposed plant matter (grass clippings, leaves, coffee grounds, fruits, and veggies) also makes a fine mulch. Neither sawdust nor animal-based materials should be used as a mulch, nor should you use a plastic liner under the mulch layer, as it will restrict water movement and limit oxygen availability in the root area.

TRANSPLANTING MATURE TREES

If you want to landscape with mature trees and can't wait for young ones to grow, consider hiring a mechanical tree spade company. The tree contractor will know the best time of year to transplant your tree.

Generally, a tree over 10 feet tall or with a root ball greater than 3 feet in diameter usually requires mechanical planting. A tree spade is a mechanical device used to dig and transplant trees. The spade encircles the tree, and large blades are forced into the ground diagonally around the tree to form a root ball. There are various sizes of tree spades, because the size of the ball must be proportional to the tree size. Generally, the width of the root ball is a minimum of 10 inches in diameter per inch of trunk diameter.

When the planting hole is dug with a spade, the sides of the hole

Mulch is a beneficial and aesthetically pleasing ground cover.

tend to glaze, which can inhibit root penetration. Be sure the sides are roughened up or loosened before the tree is planted. Trees greater than 4 inches in diameter are sometimes supported by **guying**, a technique used to secure large trees by wires, and provides stronger support than staking.

strength of the tree. Leaves smaller than normal and stunted twig growth are signs of stress or poor health. Finally, check for insect damage and disease. Has there been excessive defoliation or dieback in the crown?

All of these factors are important because they will determine how you will prune the tree. By removing branches, you are removing some of the tree's ability to produce energy through photosynthesis, a process that involves the leaves converting energy into nutrients for the plant. Also, there is food stored in the branches that will be lost when they are pruned.

Keep this in mind when pruning, because although trees can be very resilient, you may send a stressed tree into a downward spiral with a severe pruning and kill the tree.

Consider the following issues in order to ensure that your tree is pruned properly and remains healthy and aesthetically pleasing:

- Know what kind of tree you are going to prune.
- Know the growth habits and the tree's natural shape and appearance, in order to maintain shape.
- Know how to make a proper cut.
- What are your objectives for pruning?
- What tools will you need?

ABOVE: Hand pruners or secateurs are used on small trees for cuts up to ½ inch in diameter.

RIGHT: Here are some of the main tools required for pruning: secateurs, pruning saw, pole saw, and pole pruner. They require some basic maintenance to function well. Keep them clean, sharp, and oiled.

- What time of year is it?
- Is it a young tree or a mature tree?

Pruning tools

In order to prune your trees and shrubs properly and efficiently, use the following recommended tools.

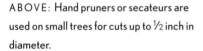

Basic pruning tools include pruning shears (or secateurs), lopping shears, a pruning saw (or handsaw), a pole pruner, and a pole saw. These tools are available at most hardware and gardening centers.

- **Pruning shears**—Hand pruners, or secateurs, are used on small trees and shrubs to make cuts up to $^1/_2$ inch in diameter. The best are the bypass-style pruning shears. These shears have a curved blade that cuts by passing against a curved bill. Anvil-style shears have a straight blade, which when cut against a flat anvil, can crush branch tissue and leave stubs, and are not recommended. To make a proper cut, always place the blade close to the parent stem and cut upward. When pruning back to a bud, make the cut $^1/_4$ inch above the active bud at the same angle as the bud. If you cut any closer, the bud will dry out. If you cut any higher, a stub is left, subjecting the branch to dieback.
- **Lopping shears**—These are used in the same way as hand shears, but they have longer handles and can cut branches up to $1\,^1/_4$

inches in diameter. Lopping shears work well for cutting out old canes (woody stems) to rejuvenate the plant.

- A **pruning saw (handsaw)** is necessary for pruning small trees. Use it to cut branches greater than 1 to 1 1/2 inches in diameter. A handsaw has a 13- or 14-inch tri-cut blade that is very sharp and provides a fast, clean cut with the least effort. When the saw is dull, simply replace the blade. Wear leather gloves when using a pruning saw and be careful to avoid cutting yourself with this razor-sharp blade.

- A **pole pruner** is a great tool that allows you to prune branches that cannot be reached from the ground. A pole pruner can make small cuts near branch ends that would be awkward with a handsaw. It should have a bypass-style pruner head, similar to that of hand shears. The pole length can range from 6 to 10 feet, and extensions are available to reach other heights. You should not use a pole pruner to cut any more than the head will allow, usually 1 to 1 1/2 inches. Also try to avoid cutting deadwood with it, as it is hard on the blade.

- Another useful pole tool is the **pole saw**. It uses the same tri-cut blade as the handsaw for a fast, clear cut. Use it to prune branches larger

TOP: A pruning saw is a tool necessary for pruning small trees. It can cut branches greater than 1 1/2 inches in diameter.

FAR LEFT: A pole pruner allows you to prune branches that cannot be reached from the ground using other tools. The pole can range from 6 to 10 feet.

A pole saw is another useful tool when reaching into the canopy. You should wear gloves, protective eyewear, and a helmet when you are pruning larger branches over your head.

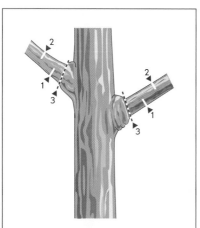

The three-cut method prevents the bark from tearing. A proper cut just outside the branch collar is necessary for the third cut.

than 1 1/2 inches in diameter to remove deadwood, and to prune stubs and broken branches.

When using pole tools, avoid cutting large branches directly over your head. Keep your cuts small and manageable, and let an arborist handle the bigger pruning jobs.

If the type of pruning you're doing requires the use of a small chainsaw, you should also consider hiring an arborist. Chainsaws are dangerous tools best left to skilled professionals.

Keep your tools clean and sharp so that they will leave clean, accurate cuts. Dull tools will leave a ragged appearance and could damage the bark. When pruning diseased branches you will have to sterilize your tools between cuts to avoid spreading the disease throughout the tree or to other trees. Use disinfectants such as Lysol, alcohol, or bleach. Dilute them in a 1-to-10 ratio with water and spray the tools or dip them in the solution. In both cases, be sure to completely cover the entire tool to properly disinfect it. These solutions can cause tools to rust, so carefully rinse or dry your tools after use and oil them when stored. Choose good quality tools and maintain them, and your pruning jobs will be much easier.

Proper pruning technique

Use your secateurs (or pruning shears) to remove branches and other plant parts up to 1/2 inch in diameter. Prune small branches 1/4 inch above an outward-facing bud to direct new growth away from the canopy interior.

When pruning a larger branch with a handsaw, three cuts are necessary to avoid having the weight of the branch tear the bark at the point where the branch meets the main stem: an undercut, followed by an overcut, then the final cut. ISA practice recommends the following steps:

1. The first cut undercuts the limb 1 or 2 feet out from the parent branch or trunk. Cut only one-third of the way through the branch. The undercut prevents the bark from stripping.
2. The next step is to make a top cut slightly farther out on the limb. Cut clear through to remove the branch. The limb will drop smoothly when the weight is released.
3. The final cut removes the stub. It should be clean and straight. It is important that this cut is made properly so the tree can seal over the wound. Look for the natural swelling where the branch

CODIT stands for compartmentalization of decay in trees. When a wound is created in a tree, for example by pruning, the tree has the ability to prevent decay from spreading. The tree forms four barriers that prevent decay from spreading inward, outward, vertically, and horizontally. This ability is unique to trees, therefore pruning paint isn't recommended or required.

meets the main stem. This is called the branch bark ridge. Slightly out from that is the **branch collar** where the cut should be made, leaving a small neat shoulder that protrudes just beyond the ridge. Do not leave a large stub or cut too close. A flush cut will create a bigger wound than necessary and won't seal over.

Start any pruning job by removing deadwood. Deadwood is easy to spot during the growing season because it bears no leaves and snaps easily, revealing no green under the bark. After removing deadwood, prune your trees to improve their structure, making them stronger and more attractive.

A thinning cut removes a branch at the junction of the stem or parent limb, or shortens a primary branch to a lateral shoot large enough to assume **apical dominance** (to support life). The remaining lateral should have the diameter of at least one-third the diameter of the portion being removed (the remaining part of the branch should be at least one-third the size of the portion removed).

Pruning young trees

Pruning at the time of planting is not recommended, except to remove broken branches and deadwood. If necessary, a central trunk or leader should be developed by removing competing leaders. Do not cut back to compensate for root loss. Do not remove lower branches or perform any crown thinning until the tree is established.

If young trees are trained or pruned to promote good structure, they will likely remain vibrant for longer than trees that have not been similarly pruned. Defects can be removed, a single dominant leader can be selected, and branches can be spaced out well along the main trunk. Well-pruned young trees have a lower potential for structural failure at maturity and require less maintenance later on.

CONIFEROUS EVERGREENS

Coniferous evergreens don't readily produce new shoots from old wood. Pruning beyond the foliage into older wood will result in dieback and decline. Limit pruning to the portion of the crown that has foliage. The best time to prune evergreens is while they are actively growing or while new growth is still soft.

Pine and spruce need little pruning. Remove deadwood and co-dominant leaders (see glossary). If you want a dense, compact appearance, you must "candle" the tree. Before the needles come out, head back the new shoots on pines with hand shears or by pinching off the shoots. If you want compact growth on your spruce, head back the terminal and side branches to buds in late winter, or early spring, before new growth emerges.

The lower branches on the trunk of a young tree help develop a strong trunk and proper trunk taper. Leave them on for the first 4 or 5 years before pruning them to the lowest permanent branch.

The process of training young trees, as recommended by the International Society of Arborists in its *Arborists' Certification Study Guide,* includes five simple steps.

1. Remove broken, dead, dying, or damaged branches.
2. Select and establish a dominant leader. There should be only one leader, usually the strongest vertical stem. Competing stems should be cut back or removed.
3. Select and establish the lowest permanent branch. The height of this branch should be determined by the location and intended function of the tree.
4. Select and establish scaffold branches, the permanent and structural branches of your tree. Choose based on good attachment, appropriate size, and spacing in relation to other branches.
5. Select temporary branches below the lowest permanent branch. These branches should be retained temporarily because they help provide energy back to the trunk and provide shade to young trunk tissues. Smaller temporary branches can be left intact because they help form good trunk taper, which provides stability for the tree. Larger branches should be pruned.

This training process should be spread out over many years, if practical. A widely accepted goal is to remove no more than 25 percent of the canopy in any one year. Proper training can be accomplished by removing much less.

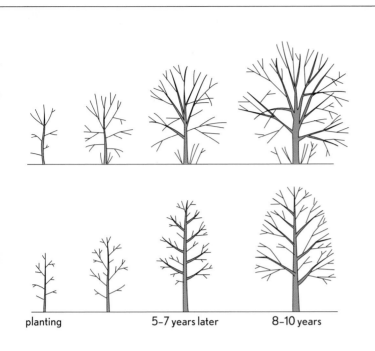

before

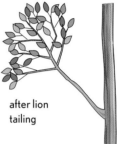

after lion
tailing

Training your trees by corrective pruning is the best way to maintain and ensure proper structure and health of your trees. It is better to make smaller cuts when the trees are young than to try to correctively prune a mature tree.

Pruning mature trees

Factors to consider when pruning mature trees include site, time of year, species, size, growth habit, vitality, and maturity. As a general rule, mature trees are less tolerant of severe pruning than young ones. Large, mature trees should require little routine pruning. The older and larger a tree becomes, the less energy it has in reserve to close wounds and defend against decay or insect attack. The pruning

Proper thinning of a branch involves maintaining well-spaced limbs so there is an even distribution of foliage along the whole branch. By removing too many inner and lower branches and foliage on a limb, too much weight is concentrated on the ends, and branch taper is discouraged. This makes for a weak branch that is prone to failure during storms. This poor practice is referred to as "lion tailing" and should be avoided.

Periodic pruning for specific purposes such as deadwood, branch spacing, interfering limbs, poor branch unions, etc., make for healthy and beautiful trees. The benefits of such activity are seen after a tree has been properly pruned.

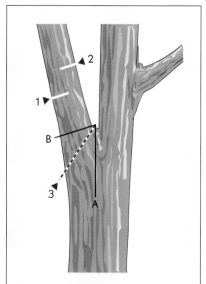

When removing a co-dominant stem or V-shaped crotch, first remove most of the stem by under-cutting it, followed by a top cut. The angle of your first cut should bisect the angle formed by the branch bark ridge (B), and an imaginary line made perpendicular to the growth of the leader being removed.

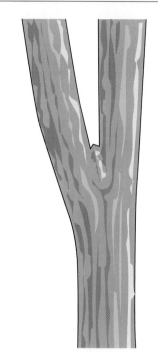

Co-dominant stems have a weak point of attachment and are prone to failure. Remove or cut back the stems, preferably when the tree is young.

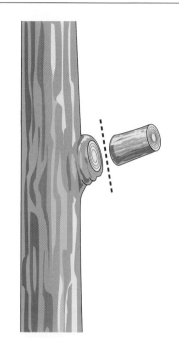

To prune a dead stub, cut the stub back to the collar of living tissue, removing only the dead portion.

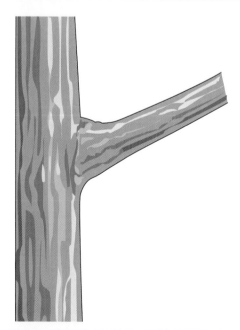

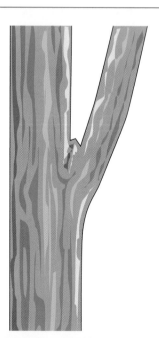

A wider crotch angle or a U-shaped crotch is stronger than a narrow V-shaped crotch. A V-shape crotch is weaker, more likely to break, and may have included bark.

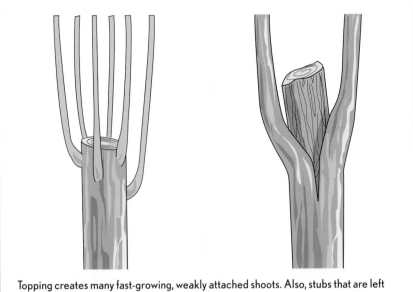

Topping creates many fast-growing, weakly attached shoots. Also, stubs that are left from topping will decay and rot.

of mature trees is usually limited to removal of dead branches to reduce the severity of structural defects.

Pruning tips: What *not* to do

Topping trees is the worst form of pruning possible. It involves cutting back tree branches to stubs or lateral branches that are not large enough to assume dominance. Topping is harmful and will negatively impact the health, structure, and maintenance of your trees. Commonly, homeowners want to top their trees because they feel they have become too large and may damage a home or other structures. Nevertheless, topping trees creates more hazard in the long run.

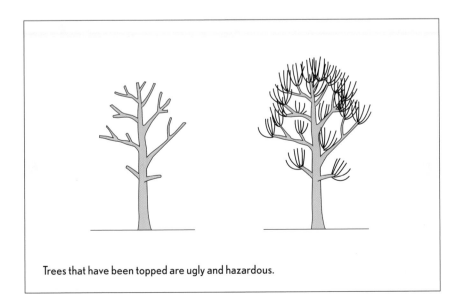

Trees that have been topped are ugly and hazardous.

OPPOSITE: Head back new shoots or candles on evergreens if you want a compact appearance.

Topping disfigures trees. The tree's natural branching structure is destroyed and will never fully regain its natural form. When a topped tree is without leaves during the dormant winter months it looks unsightly. With leaves it is simply a dense ball of foliage, lacking a nice flowing shape.

Topping depletes the tree of stored energy reserves and reduces the tree's ability to produce energy, as a large percentage of the leaves are removed. The stressed tree will form a growth of multiple shoots below each topping cut. These shoots grow quickly, are very weak, and are prone to breaking in the wind. Also, stubs left from topping usually decay, causing wood to rot.

Severely topped trees are more susceptible to insect and disease infestations. The bark can also be damaged by the sun, causing **cankers,** bark splitting, and the death of some branches.

Topping will cost you money in the long run: topping is high maintenance as it will need to be done every couple of years. If the tree dies, it will have to be removed. If weak growth is damaged in a storm, it will need to be cleaned up. As well, the value of your property will be reduced, as disfigured, topped trees are considered an expense.

Another pruning method to avoid is called **lion tailing**, which involves stripping branches of their lateral limbs, leaving growth only on the ends of the branches. This depletes energy reserves and discourages proper taper and diameter growth of the limb. It also concentrates weight on the ends of the branches, increasing their risk of failure during storms.

A **flush cut** removes a branch right to the trunk, leaving no stub at all. Never cut any branch flush. Flush cuts remove the natural protection zones a tree needs to prevent invasion by insect pests and disease.

Stub cuts, the opposite of flush cuts, can be just as harmful. A stub is what remains of a branch after the cut. Long or short, dead stubs are a fuel source for disease and a safe harbour for insects.

Do not apply pruning paint to a wound after a pruning cut. When a proper pruning cut is made, the tree has a natural ability to compartmentalize the wound and prevent decay from entering it in any direction. The tree's cambium layer will then produce **callus** tissue around and over the wound. When pruning a stub that has formed callus tissue, only the dead portion of the stub should be removed, preserving the healthy callus.

Pruning shrubs

Shrub pruning is very similar to shade tree pruning. Start by removing dead, dying, and diseased branches. Then make thinning cuts to remove some of the older stems or canes. This will encourage younger sprouts from the root crown, which will be more vigorous and produce more flowers. Heading cuts that pertain only to shrub

After pruning, you will need to remove brush that has been cut. Some wood, such as cedar, is excellent for making garden structures such as arbors or furniture.

pruning may be necessary to shape the plant, and will control and direct growth. Heading cuts must be made at a lateral branch or a bud. Head back to a lateral or a bud that points in the direction you want the plant to grow. If you want a more spreading plant, cut back to an outward-facing bud or lateral. For an upright plant, cut back to an inward-facing bud.

Prune spring-flowering shrubs once the flowers have died. Prune summer- or fall-flowering shrubs during dormancy.

Certain shrubs that have grown too large can be trained into small trees, such as the amur maple, the Russian olive, and the smoke bush. Remove their lower branches and tidy their interior.

Shearing versus pruning

Shearing removes a portion of the current season's growth and is done one or more times per year. This gives a structured formal, hard appearance as foliage is concentrated on the perimeter of the plant. The dense outer canopy reduces light and air penetration. If a portion of the plant became damaged, ugly holes could appear due to a lack of foliar growth (presence of leaves) within the plant.

Pruning removes plant parts prior to the current growth season. This tends to rejuvenate the plant. It also provides a more natural shape and improves overall health.

Some shrubs can be grown as small multi-stemmed trees by selecting major stems to become trunks and pruning the lower branches to the height wanted.

A shrub may need renovation when all new foliage is tall, bare stems.

Shrub renovation

A shrub may need renovation when
- it has been neglected and has grown too large;
- it is flowering too high;
- it is too sprawling and takes up too much room;
- all new foliage is tall bare stems.

Shearing your shrubs gives them a structured formal appearance.

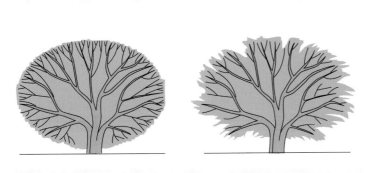

These are the growth habits of sheared and pruned shrubs. Shearing provides a more formal appearance, while pruned shrubs have a more natural, informal appearance.

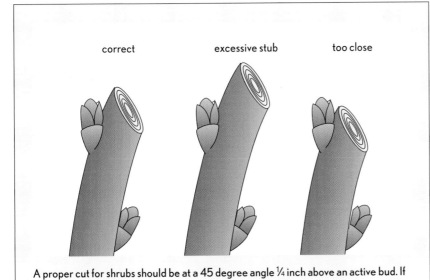

correct   excessive stub   too close

A proper cut for shrubs should be at a 45 degree angle ¼ inch above an active bud. If the cut is too close, it will interfere with bud growth and dry out. If too far out, the branch will die back.

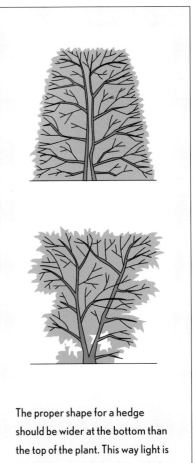

The proper shape for a hedge should be wider at the bottom than the top of the plant. This way light is available to the whole plant to help keep it full and dense.

To renovate a shrub, head back the entire plant to 6 to 12 inches above the ground. Renovating in early spring before buds break will result in rapid plant regrowth.

Hedges

Prune hedges so the plants are wide at the bottom and narrow at the top. This will allow light to reach the lower foliage and result in healthier plants. This method also minimizes the potential for snow and ice loading.

Begin pruning when hedge plants are young to assure a desirable shape. Hedges can be maintained by shearing or pruning.

Chapter 5

DIAGNOSING PLANT PROBLEMS

Once you have taken the time to choose your tree, plant it carefully in an appropriate space, and carry out tasks such as mulching and watering, you are ready to enjoy its spectacular natural beauty for years to come. You have made an investment that will benefit your community and increase the monetary and aesthetic value of your home.

However, your tree's strength and vigor can be compromised by factors such as stress, disease, or insects. Although most trees will thrive in a yard if properly cared for, you should be on the lookout for any irregularities in your tree's health. To be healthy, a tree requires sufficient water and sufficient light, and a proper balance of nutrients. Trees cope with environmental stresses such as shading and competition for water and nutrients within their native environment by adjusting their growth and development patterns according to the resources available. When you see changes in your tree's appearance, carefully examine the problem. By identifying specific symptoms of damage and finding the cause, you can then decide how to treat it.

Biotic and abiotic plant problems

Plant health problems fall into two basic categories: biotic and abiotic. **Biotic** problems are caused by living agents such as insects, mites, animals, and diseases such as fungi, bacteria, and viruses. They are considered infectious because they can spread from one tree to the next.

Non-living agents (abiotic) are non-infectious. **Abiotic** disorders are caused by weather conditions, soil conditions, and man-made physical and chemical disturbances to the air and environment. Stress resulting from abiotic disorders can weaken plants and leave them susceptible to biotic disorders. Abiotic disorders comprise the

There are two categories of plant health problems: biotic and abiotic problems. Living agents such as insects, mites, animals, and diseases such as fungi, bacteria, and viruses cause biotic problems. Biotic problems are infectious. Abiotic problems are caused by weather and soil conditions, and man-made physical and chemical disturbances to the air and environment. Abiotic problems are non-infectious, but they comprise the majority of tree health problems.

Insufficient soil drainage can prove to be fatal. The tree will become unstable and, in some cases, topple over, because its anchoring roots have rotted.

Stress from drought can cause leaves to appear lackluster, change their color, and drop early.

majority of tree health problems. In fact, 70 to 90 percent of all plant problems are the result of environmental conditions such as soil compaction, high or low temperatures, drought, air pollution, nutrient deficiencies, herbicides, root collar disorders, mechanical injury, flooding, and poor species selection. Often, plant health problems can be a combination of infectious and non-infectious problems.

How to make a diagnosis

Proper diagnosis starts with careful examination.

Excessive water sprouts are an indicator of stress.

- Start by correctly identifying the plant. This should help establish whether your tree's growth rate is normal or not. Also, many biotic and abiotic conditions are specific to certain tree types.
- The next step is to examine the site. Consider the area the tree is growing in. Are soil and drainage adequate? Has there been any activity that has changed the site by changing the grade or compacting the soil? What were the recent climate conditions? Drought, excessive rain, and extreme temperature fluctuation can all influence tree health. Were any pesticides used recently or in previous years? What was growing on the site previously? Were those plants also experiencing problems? Could the same problems be affecting the current plants?
- Note symptoms by looking at leaves, shoots, roots, and the root collar. You will often notice changes to foliage first. Examine the growth and color of your tree's leaves. Yellow-green foliage can be indicative of nutrient deficiencies. Dead leaves at the top of the tree are usually the result of mechanical or environmental root stress. Twisted and curled leaves could be caused by herbicides or insects. Look for insects and evidence of insects, such as chewing,

Correct diagnosis of plant problems requires a careful examination of the situation. The ISA recommends the following tips:

- Accurately identify the plant, because many insects and disease are plant specific.
- Look for a pattern of abnormality.
- Carefully examine the landscape for other existing problems.
- Examine the roots of your tree for any discoloration.
- Check the trunk and branches for wounds that provide entrance for pathogens.
- Note the portion and appearance of affected leaves.

The treatment method used for a particular insect or disease problem will depend on the species involved, the extent of the problem, and a variety of other factors specific to the situation and local regulations. Always consult a professional if you have any doubt about the nature of the problem or proper treatment.

mining, skeletonizing, and insect waste (such as honeydew). Root tips should be white and fleshy. Brown and black tips indicate overly wet soil or the presence of root-rotting organisms.

- Examine the trunk and branches. Look for wounds, blisters, cankers, insects feeding, or any abnormalities. Low wounds can result from mechanical damage by lawn mowers or string trimmers. Small holes can indicate the presence of **boring** insects. Weather can cause sunscald or frost cracks, and rodents can chew and damage bark. Excessive water sprouts and sucker growth can indicate stress on the tree from severe pruning or poor growing conditions. Examine how the trunk enters the soil. If the trunk flare isn't evident, the tree may be planted too deep. If the trunk is flat or indented on one side, it probably has a girdling root.

Insects

Most insects found in the yard do not damage ornamental trees and shrubs. Many insects are considered beneficial because they help with pollination or prey on other damage-causing insects. Often an insect problem will be secondary to problems brought on by stress or disease. Killing all insects, without regard to their kind and function, can be detrimental to tree health.

However, most tree species have at least one pest that causes damage. Many of the serious pests attacking ornamental plants in North America were imported by accident on plant material. The gypsy moth, the elm leaf beetle, the Japanese beetle, and the European elm bark beetle are all imported pests.

Insects can cause damage by boring into the tree, chewing the leaves, and sucking the sap from leaves.

Boring insects are chewing insect larvae that tunnel under a tree's bark and into the wood. These near-invisible pests affect twigs, limbs, and trunks. Look for small holes in the branches or trunks where the insects enter, which may be accompanied by bits of sawdust nearby. Boring insects eat inner bark, phloem, and xylem, disrupting the flow of water and nutrients from the roots to the canopy, which causes considerable damage to healthy trees. Young trees and softwood types are particularly vulnerable.

Borers are likely to attack trees that are already weakened, and can be considered a secondary problem. Symptoms of borer damage are a thin crown, crown dieback, and a noticeable decline in plant vigor. Examples of boring inserts are the bronze birch borer and the European bark beetle.

Chewing insects, or defoliators, eat plant tissue such as leaves, flowers, buds, and twigs. Some will eat the entire leaf, and others will skeletonize the leaf by eating the tissue between its veins, or hollow out the leaf, feeding between the leaf surfaces. These last are called leaf miners. A healthy deciduous tree can withstand complete defoliation in one season; however, complete defoliation two years in a row could seriously harm it. Conifers will often die after one defoliation. Keep trees that have had heavy defoliation well watered and mulched, and make sure the required nutrients are available in the soil.

Common defoliators include caterpillars such as the gypsy moth and the Eastern tent caterpillar, sawflies, leaf beetles, Japanese beetles, birch leaf miners, and cedar leaf miners.

Damage-causing insects fall into three categories: boring insects such as the European bark beetle, chewing insects such as the gypsy moth and the Eastern tent caterpillar, and sucking insects such as aphids and mites.

1. Larva wood borers and adult
2. Leaf-chewing insect damage
3. Bark beetle
4. Mites
5. Lace bug
6. Scale insects
7. Tent caterpillar egg mass
8. Aphids
9. Serpentine leafminers
10. Root-feeding white grub

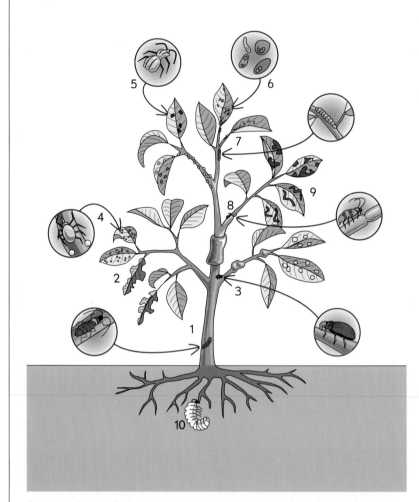

Sometimes insects that cause damage to trees can be seen doing the damage, but in many cases the damage is more visible than the pest. This is because some pests, such as spider mites, are too small to see, or , by the time damage is detected, the insects may be gone.

Sucking insects have piercing mouthparts that penetrate leaves, twigs, branches, flowers, or fruit and then feed on the plant's juices by sucking out the sap. Signs of such damage include fading leaf color, curling and twisting leaves, wilting foliage, and malformed flowers. Some common sucking insects are aphids, leafhoppers, mites, mealybugs, and scales. Aphids can secrete a sugary substance called honeydew, which attracts ants and flies and is a nuisance when it covers objects located beneath branches. Honeydew also promotes the growth of sooty mold, a black and unsightly fungus. Heavy infestations of aphids will stunt tree growth.

Mites, often referred to as spider mites, are arachnids. They can cause foliage bronzing and leaf drop. Mites reproduce rapidly in hot, dry weather. Because they are very small and hard to see, diagnose mites by holding a white sheet of paper under a branch and shaking

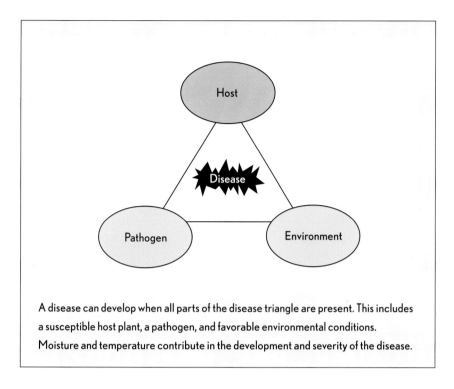

A disease can develop when all parts of the disease triangle are present. This includes a susceptible host plant, a pathogen, and favorable environmental conditions. Moisture and temperature contribute in the development and severity of the disease.

it. Mites will land on the paper and can be seen crawling about. A heavy infestation of spider mites, active during the summer months, will leave silvery webbing in the affected area.

Diseases

Diseases in trees and shrubs can reduce the health of the plant, decrease life expectancy, and mar the beauty of the landscape. Infectious diseases are contagious and are caused by living organisms called pathogens. Pathogens are parasitic and weaken the host tree by absorbing food from it for their own use.

Most tree diseases are caused by fungi, but other pathogens include bacteria and viruses. For disease to occur, three conditions are necessary: the availability of a host plant susceptible to infection; the presence of a pathogen; and favorable environmental conditions. By managing one or more of these components, you can reduce the amount of disease. Temperature and moisture are key factors in disease development. Moisture activates most pathogens and aids their spread, and each pathogen has an optimal temperature range for development. Pathogens are spread by wind, rain, animals, insects, and contaminated tools.

Plants can respond to infectious diseases in many ways, although the most obvious signs appear on foliage. Most leaf diseases are caused by fungi. Fungus attacks new shoots and leaves in spring, causing them to turn brown and die. In older leaves, it causes brown patches and premature leaf drop. Fungus spores require moisture to genminate, so the risks are severe during wet springs but infection is reduced in warm, dry weather. Fungus overwinters on fallen

1. Twig blight
2. Leaf spots
3. Shoot blight
4. Powdery mildew
5. Canker
6. Fruit rot
7. Wilt
8. Crown
9. Root knots
10. Root rot

Disease symptoms can be seen throughout the tree, on the leaves, fruit, branches and twigs, trunk, and roots. Symptoms provide clues to identify the disease causing the problem.

leaves and in cankers on twigs it has killed; prevention requires cutting out all dead twigs and branches and raking up fallen infected leaves.

Powdery mildew, rust, leaf spots, scab, and anthracnose are common diseases that affect foliage. The powdery mildew fungus starts as gray or white circular patches on foliage and spreads to become a powdery coating on leaves and stems. It thrives when humidity is high, especially when plants are too shaded or crowded. Symptoms of scab include scab-like lesions on the fruits and foliage of trees such as apples, crab apples, and hawthorns, which are particularly prone to scab. Trees with these problems need pruning to allow more air movement through the canopy and more light penetration.

Cankers are visible on the branches and trunk of the trees. They are a result of the bark and cambium layers dying, followed by the death of the underlying wood. The bark in these areas splits as it dries out and exposes the wood below. Most cankers are caused by fungi, although sunscald and frost crack can also cause similar wounding. Pruning branches to well below the affected area will help contain the disease.

Vascular wilts are diseases that disrupt the water-conducting elements of the plant, blocking water movement to the crown. Leaves will wilt, branches will die back, and eventually the tree will die. One example of vascular wilt is Dutch elm disease, which is spread by the elm bark beetle. The beetle acts as a carrier, carrying the fungus that causes the disease. Therefore, diseased and dead trees must be removed to control the beetle population.

Another is verticillium wilt, a fungus that inhabits surrounding soil and invades and plugs water-conducting tissue, shutting off the water supply to top growth. Common symptoms are tree wilt, and leaves that turn yellow then die. Because verticillium wilt lives in the soil, you should not plant a tree in the same area unless it is a resistant species.

Root diseases are difficult to combat because they are often hidden from sight and access. One common root disease is armillaria root rot, which invades root tissues and forms black, shoestring-like threads just beneath the roots' bark at the base of the tree and produces clusters of mushrooms at the plant's base aboveground.

The above information about insects and diseases merely touches upon the wide variety of pest problems that can affect your plants. The key is to be aware of the signs and symptoms to look for as you examine your trees.

Control measures: Cultural practices

- Select trees that are resistant to or can withstand insect and disease problems. Plant resistant varieties.
- Don't overcrowd plants.
- Plant in sunny locations with good airflow.
- Disinfect your tools.
- Choose ideal sites when planting trees.
- Maintain healthy plants by providing adequate water and nutrients, as many diseases attack trees that are already weak.
- Reduce moisture by improving drainage and watering properly. Water early in the morning so plants are not wet for long periods of time. Don't water late in the day.
- Practice good sanitation. Rake leaves and twigs under and around affected trees. Many insect and disease spores overwinter in the leaf litter. Removing and even burning leaves can help minimize disease spread.
- Consider replacing a tree that requires annual spraying of chemical pesticides with a resistant cultivar or a plant that is more suited to the site.
- Prune to allow more air and light penetration through the crown of the tree, which can reduce disease and pest problems. Physically remove pests by pruning affected growth. For

Apple scab—a fungus disease that affects the leaves and the fruit of apple and crabapple trees. The leaves and the fruit can develop spots or lesions, causing the leaves to turn yellow, die, and drop. The fruit will have brown or black spots and can be irregularly shaped. This is a very common disease and will often cause premature leaf drop, leaving the tree bare in late summer. Cool, wet weather in the spring plays a key role in the degree of infection. Proper culture practices are important in controlling this disease. The fungus overwinters in the leaves on the ground, so rake them up in the late summer and fall each year and dispose of them. Prune the tree to allow for good air circulation and light penetration. When planting, choose an open sunny area with good air movement. More importantly, *choose high-quality, disease resistant varieties.* Crabapple cultivars considered resistant to scab include Malus "Adams," Autumn Glory, Baskatong, Professor Sprenger, Red Snow, and White Cascade. The use of chemical fungicides may be necessary for persistent and severe infections. This may involve numerous applications for good control.

Black knot—a fungal disease affecting cherry and plum species. The infection causes hard black swellings on branches and small twigs up to 4 inches long. These black swellings will eventually girdle and kill the branch. In late winter or early spring, prune out and destroy the black knot. Cut approximately 2 to 3 inches below the visible signs, because the fungus may have grown internally below the black knot. Disinfect your pruning tools with bleach after every cut.

Fire blight—a bacterial disease that affects a wide range of plants in the *Rosaceae* family. This includes serviceberry, hawthorn, cherry, mountain ash, pear, apple, etc. Flowers, twigs, and branches are affected as they wilt, darken in color, and dry out and die. Dead leaves remain attached to the plant and take on a scorched appearance, which is characteristic of the disease. Fire blight may also extend into the larger branches and the trunk where cankers are formed. These cankers appear as dark, sunken areas with the presence of bacterial ooze on the surface of the cankers. This disease is spread by rain, wind, and insects. When the tree is dormant during the winter months and the tree is dry, prune out all infected branches. Cut off infected wood at least 1 foot below any discolored tissue or cankered area. Disinfect your tools after every cut with one part bleach to four parts water, as the disease is easily spread by pruning. Avoid excessive nitrogen fertilization, which will promote succulent vegetative growth, and prune lightly to avoid succulent growth as well. Lush, succulent growth is more susceptible to fire blight.

Powdery mildew—a fungus disease that produces a white to gray powdery mold on upper leaf surfaces and young tissue, usually occurring in late summer and early fall. This disease can affect lilacs, rose privet, and catalpa, as well as other woody ornamental plants. It commonly appears when warm days are followed by cool nights. Powdery mildew is more of a cosmetic problem that does not damage the plant to any great degree. However, it can be more damaging to roses, causing severe deformation. To help reduce the problem, do not overcrowd plants. Plant them in sunny locations where air movement is good. Watering during the day will reduce the spread of the disease, while overhead irrigation late in the day will increase the development and spread of the disease.

Dutch elm disease—a very destructive disease that has killed millions of elms in North America. The disease is caused by a vascular wilt fungus that blocks water flow in the tree until the tree's transpiration is completely cut off. Symptoms include the wilting of large branches. The leaves turn yellow and begin to droop, then fall off. This may begin on one side of the tree. The sapwood becomes stained a dark brown or black, and can be easily seen in twigs and branches when cut. Young trees can be killed in a few weeks, while older trees can take year or two. Old, weakened, or stressed trees are more susceptible to the disease. The disease is spread by the elm bark beetle. The beetles carry spores of the fungus from infected trees to the sapwood of healthy trees. The beetles live under the bark of dead and dying elms as well as elm logs. Diseased and dead trees must be removed and destroyed to help control the beetle population. Pruning of infected branches should be done in the fall and not in spring and summer, because this is when trees are most susceptible to new infection. A trunk injection treatment, available through trained arborists, may be helpful as well.

Diplodia tip blight—has caused a lot of problems to Austrian pines in the landscape. It will also affect most two- and three-needled pines, including red, Scotch, mugo, and ponderosa pines. The symptoms are death and flagging of young shoots. The tips or ends of branches die. This disease usually attacks pines in an already weakened state. Once again, improve tree health and vigor by watering, relieving soil compaction, and fertilizing. Also improve air circulation and avoid crowding pines. As well, avoid planting Austrian pines on sites that will be exposed to summer drought.

Cytospora canker—a fungal disease that usually affects trees in an already weakened state from the stresses of poor soil and dry sites. Spruce trees, e.g., blue spruce, Norway, and white spruce can be affected. The fungus attacks the lowest branches of the tree, working its way upward. The disease enters through wounds or dead branches. A canker is formed that eventually kills the branches by girdling. Symptoms to look for are pitch oozing from the infected branches or stems and a change of color in the needles that eventually die and fall from the tree. Prune dead and infected branches in dry weather in winter. Employ good cultural practices to help the tree become stronger and protect it from further spread of disease. Avoid damaging trunk and branches.

example, cut off a nest of fall webworm or tent caterpillar, prune out black knot from an infected cherry tree, or remove dead and diseased branches from a mountain ash infested with fire blight.

- Some diseases require alternate hosts to complete their cycle and do their damage. Hawthorn rust is a disease that affects foliage, and is characterized by reddish-brown spots on leaves. Juniper hosts and *Rosaceaus* hosts such as hawthorn combine to allow disease to spread between them and the hawthorn. In the case of hawthorn rust, the two hosts are the juniper and the hawthorn. Avoid planting different hosts in close proximity.

Control measures: Alternative pesticides

If insects and diseases cannot be controlled through cultural methods, consider user-friendly alternative pesticides that are non-toxic.

Insecticidal soap

Insecticidal soap is a contact insecticide, in that the insects must be directly sprayed to be affected. It is effective against soft-bodied insects such as aphids, whiteflies, sawflies, spider mites, and scales. The soap disrupts the cell membranes of the insects, causing dehydration and death. Foliage is cleaned with soap spray, which removes dirt and honeydew. This improves photosynthesis and reduces the appearance of nuisance insects attracted to honeydew.

Advantage: Insecticidal soap has no residual effect after it has dried.

Disadvantages: It has to be sprayed directly on to insects, so it is difficult to use on very large trees, and it is phytotoxic (interferes with gas exchange on leaf and bark) to horse chestnut, mountain ash, and Japanese maple.

Horticultural oil

Horticultural oil works mainly by suffocating insects. Horticultural oil is commonly used in sprays applied before leaf break.

Advantages: It kills most insects, is non-toxic, and works on over-wintering insects. The insect must be directly hit, and it will work on most insects in these situations.

Disadvantages: It can remove blue color foliage from an evergreen, and it can be phytotoxic to certain tree species, such as Japanese maple, amur maple, black walnut, and sugar maple. It may also cause phytotoxicity for plants under moisture stress or humid conditions.

It is important to follow the instructions on the labels of both products, and take care in using them on tree specimens that may be adversely affected. The products should always be applied carefully and safely, and according to label directions.

If possible, use the non-toxic remedies as described above.

Control measures: Chemical pesticides

If non-toxic remedies have little effect, **chemical pesticides** may be necessary to control certain persistent insect and disease problems. Fungicides and insecticides should be used only when they are absolutely necessary. Make sure you are spraying at the right time, i.e., when the insects are in vulnerable stages, and do not spray needlessly. Limit pesticide use and avoid highly toxic chemicals. Follow all safety precautions. It is best to hire a licensed applicator of chemical pesticides.

In some instances, no treatment may be possible because the damage has been done and the pest is no longer present, the damage is insignificant and requires no treatment, or an effective treatment is not available or permitted.

Remember that plant problems are a part of garden life. Their presence does not always necessitate immediate intervention. Many insect visitations come in short-lived waves triggered by weather and season, such as the first swarm of aphids in early spring. Some fungal diseases are active during damp weather, and appear only in particular seasons or in periods of wetness. The objective in pest and disease control is to combat only the kinds of problems that stay and increase. Don't panic and accept some chewed leaves—the problem will probably disappear soon. In fact, with many insects, natural predators might take care of them for you.

Most insects and diseases attack stressed trees. While it is impossible to keep all diseases and insects away from your trees, here are a few tips you can follow to maintain a healthy, stress-free tree:

- Water your tree during periods of insufficient rainfall. Nutrients are transported through trees in water, via xylem.
- Do not overwater your tree. This can cause root rot by creating conditions suitable to root-rot fungi.
- Put mulch under your tree. This prevents other plants from growing around your tree.
- Avoid soil compaction, often associated with construction activity, as it smothers the roots.
- With the exception of broken limbs, do not remove foliage from newly planted trees. Newly planted trees need all the leaves they have in order to produce energy.
- Follow recommended pruning techniques. Do not top trees, which creates entry locations for diseases and insects.
- If fungicides must be used, be sure to apply using the right method at the right time, with the right material. Follow the label carefully.

Chapter 6
PROTECTING YOUR TREES FROM DAMAGE

CONSTRUCTION AND RENOVATION

Many people buy property with dreams of constructing a beautiful home. Often they love the mature trees, which enhance both the look and value of a lot, and plans are made to build around these trees. Other homeowners may decide to add a new driveway or walkway, or undertake an ambitious home extension project. In most cases, homeowners do not realize that such activities can have serious detrimental effects on their trees. Without careful planning, trees meant to be part of a home's permanent landscape can be needlessly damaged or killed during construction.

Construction involves heavy machinery and equipment, which can break, split, and tear branches, or damage or wound trunks. Tools and supplies are often piled up at the base of a tree, causing trunk damage. Contractors unskilled in tree pruning may even remove branches that interfere with the operation of their equipment, and leave poor pruning cuts that may never seal properly.

Unfortunately, much of the damage that results from construction occurs underground, where some of the most serious harm can be done, and often cannot be immediately detected by unsuspecting homeowners. A tree's root system extends horizontally at great distances in all directions. The absorbing roots contain fine root hairs, located 6 to 12 inches under the soil. Damage to a root system causes serious harm, and can lead to the decline and death of a tree. Typical damage occurs during digging or trenching, when roots are severed or cut, or when a significant amount of the root system is removed. Roots act as stabilizers, providing anchorage and support, and trees can be rather delicate, despite their large size. If roots are damaged, branches—even the entire tree—can die. It is critical to protect roots that lie in the path of construction. Impairment of the root system will affect water and nutrient uptake and could make a tree prone to falling. Signs of stress can be visible within months, or a tree may decline over several years.

Signs of stress from root injury include

- dieback of the tips of branches, which can result in the eventual death of entire branches, usually from the top of the tree down;
- leaves that become brown and scorched on the edges from lack of water;
- stunted growth, and small or off-color leaves;
- excessive suckering or water sprout growth along the trunk and limbs (flower and seed production and water sprout formation are defense mechanisms);
- early fall color and leaf drop.

Another type of root damage occurs when soil is compacted around the root area of a tree, and soil pore spaces are greatly reduced. These pore spaces are important to tree roots because they are filled with water and air, both necessary for tree health. Soil compaction makes it hard for water to infiltrate the soil, and drainage is consequently impaired. These effects make it hard for roots to grow and function.

Adding or mounding soil or changing the grade of existing soil around a tree can also cause problems. Roots require air, space and water, so adding soil or changing a grade, even by a few inches, can smother roots by compromising their ability to access air and water.

Prevention of tree injury before and during construction

Homeowners do have options for making sure their valuable trees are not harmed during construction work. Here are some suggestions for a successful landscape protection plan as recommended by the ISA and other tree care professionals:

- When homes are built in natural or wooded areas, some trees are usually cut down to make space for building construction, and a few trees are left to surround the home. It is important to understand that these forest trees grew together, protecting one another. They grew tall and slender with high canopies because of their proximity to each other. When selected trees are cut down, other trees are exposed to intense sunlight, and leaves are exposed to the wind. A looser canopy means the trees are susceptible to sunscald on trunks and branches, and trees that grew protected by neighboring trees are more likely to be damaged in wind and by ice loading. You can avoid sun and wind stress by saving groups of trees rather than individuals. Heavily wooded

sites should be gradually thinned over two to three years to reduce shock on the remaining trees—especially if your property is located within dense pine, spruce, or fir forests.

- Get an arborist involved early, before construction begins. An arborist can determine if a tree situated in close proximity to a construction zone will survive, or if it should be removed before work begins. A skilled tree specialist can also properly prune branches that may interfere with equipment and construction before they are damaged and split or broken. Share your contractor's plans with the arborist so he or she can determine whether work can be done successfully around specific trees you want to save. Choose an arborist with experience in protecting trees from construction damage.

- Mark construction zone boundaries. Ask your builder or architect to mark areas where heavy equipment will be used.
- Make an inventory of the trees on the site. Trees that are overmature, display poor form, or have severe insect problems should be marked for removal prior to construction. Also mark trees that need pruning. Select and protect the trees you want to save.
- Erect barriers around trees, which will help preserve them. Install temporary fencing such as snow fence as far out from the trunk as possible. The minimum perimeter should be the drip line, the imaginary line around the tree that follows the edge of the tree canopy.
- Prepare the trees for construction disturbance. Minimize damage by avoiding excavation during hot, dry weather, and keep plants watered before and after digging. Prune branches that are dead, diseased, hazardous, or detrimental to the tree's shape.
- Limit machinery to one or two well-traveled routes to minimize soil compaction and damage.
- To reduce soil compaction, a good temporary measure is to spread a layer of mulch 6 to 12 inches deep in construction areas near trees and along well-traveled routes. This will distribute the weight of heavy equipment more evenly. Don't forget that the mulch must be carefully removed when the work is completed.
- Large roots severed by cutting trenches within a few feet of a tree can remove 25 to 50 percent of its root system. If trenches have to be dug near trees, consider using a tunneling technique instead. Damage to roots will be significantly reduced if tunneling is used. The process is more expensive and time consuming than trenching, but trees will be much better off.
- Take great care to sever as few roots as possible and to do so as cleanly as possible—cleanly cut roots regenerate faster than roots torn during construction.
- Not all contractors are concerned about the trees on job sites. The more protection you have in place, the better. Convey the importance of tree preservation to the people doing the work. Plan to be at the site as often as possible so you can monitor activity, or have an arborist work with the contractor to ensure tree protection.
- Sometimes contractors are allowed to burn waste materials on job sites. Be sure to designate an area well away from your trees, as smoke and heat from fire can damage the trees significantly.
- Sidewalks and driveways located too close to a tree endanger its health and may threaten pavement stability. Frost heaving, poor drainage, and pavement flaws may occur.
- Minimize root disruption by using alternative paving materials. In some communities, brick or flagstone walkways on sand foundations can be substituted for concrete.

Post-construction repair and maintenance

- Prune any broken or torn limbs. If a tree's trunk has been damaged and bark is loose and hanging, trace back to the edge of the live cambium layer with a clean cut. Consider applying lac balsam, which is a natural substance, to exposed trunk wood. Although the paste has no proven health benefits, it can serve as a cosmetic repair.
- It is very important to water your trees regularly during construction. Be sure drainage is adequate and water does not sit or pool around trees, which can deprive roots of oxygen and have the same effects as compacted soil.
- Consider hiring an arborist to help relieve compacted soil around trees. A common method called vertical mulching involves drilling holes 2 to 4 inches in diameter every few feet to a depth of approximately 12 inches, and backfilling with organic matter such as compost or peat moss. **Vertical mulching** greatly helps soil aeration.
- If trees don't have mulch around them already, add some to help retain moisture.
- Fertilizing shortly after construction is not recommended, as

SIGNS THAT INDICATE YOUR TREE COULD BE HAZARDOUS

When walking around your property or sitting and enjoying your yard, look at your trees for possible defects that could cause them to become a hazard. A tree becomes a hazard when it has defects and there is a target, such as a building or people, that it could hit if it were to fall. The tree hazard checklist as recommended by the ISA and National Arborist Association, includes the following:

- Look around the base of the tree at the soil. Make sure the soil hasn't heaved, or that the tree hasn't become partially uprooted in a heavy wind.

- Look for cracks or splits on the trunk or branches. They can form from heavy twisting and bending caused by a severe storm. Cracks will dry out and become brittle, and can lead to decay and rot.

- Look for large pieces of deadwood or hangers. Hangers are branches that have broken or torn and are hanging precariously in the canopy and could fall out at any time.

- Look for cavities or wounds. These can be serious, as tree strength at this time is reduced. Also, cankers caused by fungi or bacteria should be cause for concern. Cankers are seen as a sunken, dead area on the bark of the trunk or branches. They are a sign of decay.

- A good indicator that rot and decay are present is fruiting bodies, such as mushrooms.

- Decay and rot are cause for concern because they will reduce the structural integrity of the tree. An abundance of carpenter ants is another indicator of decayed wood.

- Look for proper trunk flare and taper. A tree should have a flare to it as it goes below ground. If it looks like a hydro pole, it is planted too deep and has poor taper, or the grade has been changed around it.

- A tree with a girdling root problem will have a sunken or indented trunk on the side where the root is being girdled. A girdling root could kill the tree. This is a common problem with Norway maples.

- Trees with co-dominant stems, poor crotch angles, included bark, and multiple branch attachments at one point are defects and should be corrected through pruning or possible by cabling and/or bracing.

Be wary of these signs when looking at your tree and consult an arborist if your tree becomes potentially hazardous.

trees have been under stress and need time to recover.

- Monitor your trees for signs of decline and hazards such as large amounts of deadwood, excessive dieback, and structural defects such as cavities or decay. Some trees may have to be removed, even if preservation efforts were made during the construction period. Monitor a tree's annual growth. A slightly damaged plant will grow more slowly and be less resistant to insects, diseases, and weather changes.
- Tree death may occur shortly after construction or years later. If your tree does not leaf out the following year, it is dead. Large trees should be carefully removed by professionals so as not to damage the remaining plants. Tree loss can have a dramatic impact on site appearance. Prompt replacement will minimize your loss.

STORM DAMAGE AND EXTREME WEATHER CONDITIONS

Storms of all shapes and sizes often wreak havoc upon trees throughout North America. The greatest dangers during a storm are property damage and physical harm that can occur when big trees fall. Preparing trees for inclement weather is advisable and should be done well in advance of the stormy season in your area.

Consult a tree professional before the storm season in your area. Ask the arborist to look for potential hazards, such as stress cracks and weak branches. Examine your trees for the following warning signs:

- Electrical wires in contact with tree branches
- Dead or partially attached limbs that could fall and cause damage or injury
- Cracked stems and branch forks that could split and cause the dramatic decline of a tree section
- Hollow or decayed areas on the trunk or main limbs, or mushrooms growing from the bark, which indicate a decayed and weakened stem
- Peeling bark and gaping wounds in the trunk, which also indicate structural weaknesses
- Fallen or uprooted trees putting pressure on other trees beneath them
- Mounded soil at the tree base, which is an indicator of a potentially unsound root system

Trees are living things and their integrity and stability changes over time. Follow proper pruning technique to reduce the weight and length of individual tree limbs and to minimize the tree's resistance to wind movement through the crown. Over their lifespan, growing

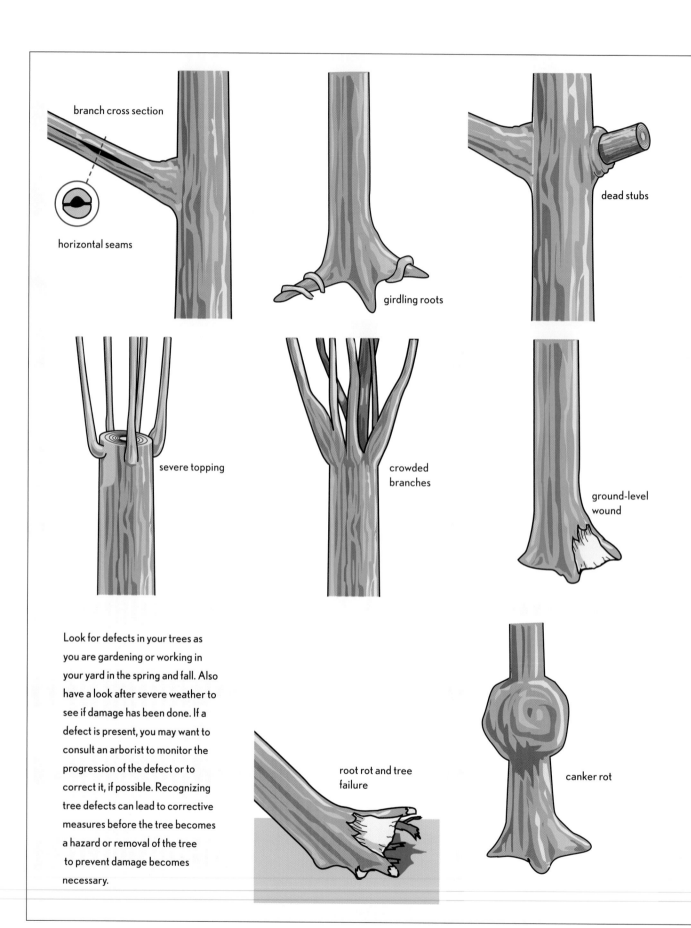

branch cross section

horizontal seams

girdling roots

dead stubs

severe topping

crowded branches

ground-level wound

Look for defects in your trees as you are gardening or working in your yard in the spring and fall. Also have a look after severe weather to see if damage has been done. If a defect is present, you may want to consult an arborist to monitor the progression of the defect or to correct it, if possible. Recognizing tree defects can lead to corrective measures before the tree becomes a hazard or removal of the tree to prevent damage becomes necessary.

root rot and tree failure

canker rot

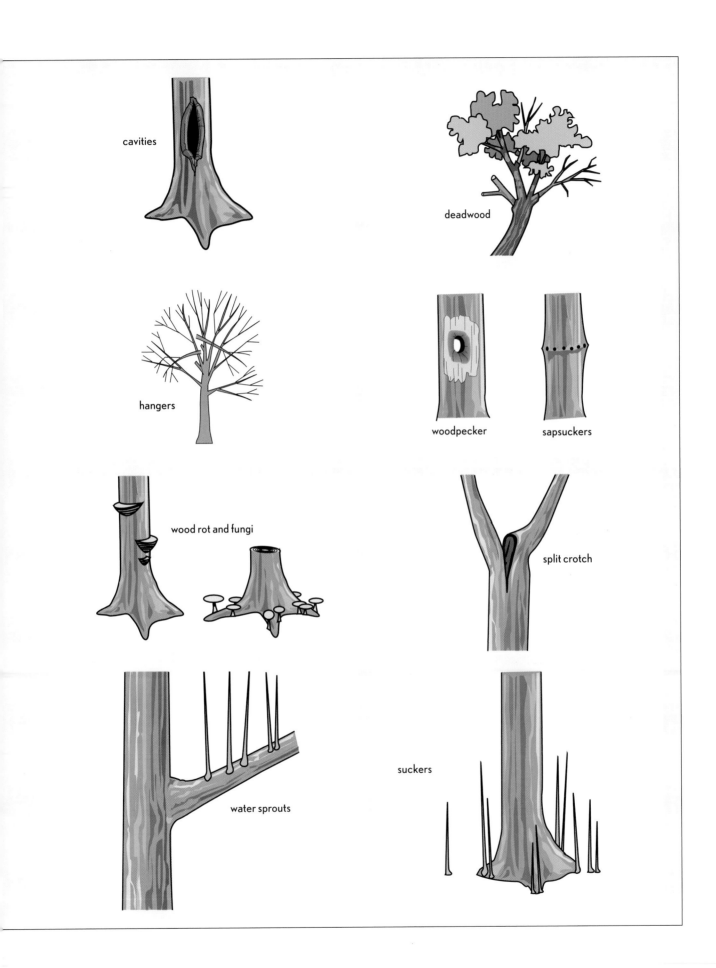

cavities

deadwood

hangers

woodpecker

sapsuckers

wood rot and fungi

split crotch

water sprouts

suckers

trees will "catch" more wind and become heavier, thus increasing the chances of limb loss and instability. Power lines, homes, and other structures that might not have been threatened a few years ago might suddenly be under threat if a tree has grown substantially.

Ensuring tree health throughout the winter

Winter conditions severely affect trees that are already stressed, so one key to preventing winter damage is keeping your trees in good health year-round.

In winter, the ground root system of a plant or tree will freeze, stopping or slowing water circulation. Evergreens are at a greater risk than other trees, because they hold their needles in the winter—the needles lose moisture to the atmosphere as well as to the plant itself. Because trees are not able to replenish lost moisture, leaves can dry out and fall off. To minimize the effects of winter drying, high-value evergreens can be treated with wax-like anti-desiccant substances that hold moisture in the leaves.

Snow and ice can become very heavy and break branches or even topple an entire tree. Pruning your tree can make it better able to withstand the extra weight of ice and snow. Mulch, too, produces a year-round benefit because it increases microbial activity and fertility of the soil underneath the tree. Mulch has the added benefit of acting as insulation between the root system and the aboveground temperature, which helps retain moisture in the root system and limits the fluctuation of soil temperature. Ensure that the ground is not frozen and has enough moisture before you add the mulch, and make sure that no more than 2 to 4 inches of an organic matter, such as wood chips, is used.

Salt used for de-icing streets and sidewalks is harmful to trees, shrubs, and grass. You can avoid damage by using only non-injurious types of de-icing salts or avoiding salt applications to sensitive areas. Some specialists feel that you can reduce salt damage by flushing the soil in treated areas with large amounts of water in the spring.

The severe ice storm of 1998 resulted in damage to many trees in eastern Canada and the northeastern United States. Ice storms are common in the region, so most trees are remarkably resilient. Trees that did not suffered major structural damage, such as split trunks, will recover over time. Trees are dormant in the winter, and damage at this time of year is less serious than if it occurs during the growing season. If a tree is reasonably healthy and only a moderate number of branches are damaged or removed, the tree should recover and in a few years will appear normal.

It is worthwhile to care for injured trees during the dormant season and wait until the growing season to see if they recover. Many young trees can bend over to ground level because of the weight of the ice collected on their crowns. Trees at this stage of development are quite flexible, and most will recover and regain an upright position when the ice melts.

It is best to wait for above-freezing temperatures to remove ice from trees. Attempting to do so while ice is still firmly attached will lead to bark damage and removal of the buds that will produce new growth in the spring.

Coniferous trees like spruces and firs generally suffer much less storm damage than deciduous species. Most coniferous species have narrow crowns and short, upright branches that minimize ice and snow loading. Damage to deciduous tree species is often much more severe. Trees with soft or brittle wood, like Manitoba maple, silver maple, native and European birches, and Siberian elm, are particularly affected. Oaks and ginkgo trees, species with strong wood and well-attached branches, suffer less structural damage.

Remember

- Safety first. The many large, broken, and ice-covered branches hanging from storm-damaged trees are extremely dangerous.
- Do not go near any injured tree close to power lines.
- Pruning large branches and stems is difficult and hazardous and should be carried out only by trained and experienced arborists.

Chapter 7

WHEN AND HOW TO HIRE AN ARBORIST

An arborist is a specialist in the care of individual trees, a skilled professional who is trained in the art and science of planting and maintenance. Arborists are knowledgeable about the needs of trees, and are trained and equipped to provide proper care. Hiring an arborist is an important decision for a homeowner to make, because proper tree care is an investment that can lead to substantial return. Well-cared-for trees are attractive and can add considerable value to your property. On the other hand, poorly maintained trees can be a significant liability. Because pruning and removing trees can be dangerous, major tree work should be undertaken only by those trained and equipped to work safely in your garden.

Services provided

It can take many years to correct improper tree care. Are you willing to take the risk? Good arborists are qualified to provide a broad range of services, including the following:

1. Pruning
   An arborist can determine what type of pruning is necessary to maintain or improve the health, appearance, and safety of your trees. Techniques include

- eliminating branches that rub against each other;
- removing limbs that interfere with wires, building facades, and windows, or obstruct streets and sidewalks;
- removing hazardous, dead, or weak limbs;
- removing diseased or insect-infested limbs;
- removing limbs damaged by adverse weather;
- thinning unnecessary branches;

Arborists provide a variety of tree care services including

- preventative maintenance to keep your tree in good health, which will help it fend off insects and disease problems;
- fertilization and advice regarding the nutritional needs of your tree;
- aeration to improve root growth and alleviate soil compaction;
- cabling and bracing for added support to branches with weak attachments;
- installation of lightening protection systems;
- spraying or injecting pesticides to control certain insect and disease problems.

Certain pruning requirements are best accomplished by professional arborists. These include eliminating large branches that rub against each other, removing large limbs that interfere with wires or houses, removing hazardous deadwood, and correcting poor V-shaped crotches.

If you own property with trees for any length of time you will likely require the services of an arborist. Their unique knowledge and skills are required to provide many specialized services. Arborists have the necessary equipment and experience to safely handle the most challenging job. In addition to these skills, they are highly valued for their consulting abilities, reports and assessments, tree preservation, expert diagnosis, and working in conjunction with landscape architects and other trades people.

- creating better structure to lessen wind resistance and reduce the potential for storm damage;
- training young trees;
- improving shape or silhouette.

Pruning mature trees usually involves climbing into the trees to make cuts. It is not safe to try to prune a tree from a ladder yourself. An arborist will climb into the tree using safety equipment. In addition to general pruning of interfering limbs and dead, dying, and diseased limbs, an arborist can provide specialty pruning such as vista pruning, crown restoration, and crown thinning.

Vista pruning involves removing branches to allow a specific view. For example, trees can be pruned to open up a view of the lake from the deck of your cottage. The intent of this type of pruning is to provide a view rather than to maintain a tree, but arborists will make every effort to minimize negative effects to tree health and appearance.

Crown restoration helps to improve the structure, form, and overall appearance of a tree that has been disfigured through severe pruning, vandalism, or storm damage. It usually involves pruning gradually over a period of time to help restore the tree to proper growth.

Crown thinning involves the selective removal of branches to increase light penetration and air movement. This type of pruning can help direct desired sunshine onto a backyard pool or patio. As well, crown thinning decreases wind resistance and the potential for storm damage.

2. Plant Health Care/Insect and Disease Management
    If you want to reduce pest problems and have healthier trees and shrubs, but you do not have the time to tend to your plants, consider hiring an arborist. He or she can monitor specific woody plants on your property, or all of them. A specialist will be able to identify, record, and analyze what is happening with your landscape plants and will be able to detect and treat problems early before they develop into more serious issues.

    This option is particularly helpful if chemical pesticides need to be applied to control certain pests. Arborists involved with plant health care are licensed applicators and will be equipped to safely apply the pesticide. They can minimize use of chemicals by applying only when needed and at the right time to maximize effectiveness. Along with chemicals, arborists will use cultural, mechanical, and biological controls to effectively care for your plants. Combined, these techniques are referred to as **integrated pest management** (IPM) and form a systematic approach to solving insect and disease problems.

3. Tree/Stump Removal
    An arborist can help decide whether or not a tree should be removed. **Tree removal is conducted only as a last resort.** It is recommended when

    ➤ a tree is dead or dying;
    ➤ a tree is considered irreparably hazardous;
    ➤ a tree is causing obstruction that is impossible to correct through pruning;

An arborist can remove your tree stump. If not properly removed, excessive sucker growth may result.

- a tree is crowding or causing harm to other trees;
- a tree is to be replaced by a more suitable specimen;
- a tree must be removed to allow for new construction.

Removing large trees is difficult and hazardous work, involving felling techniques and specialized equipment including chainsaws. This work requires an arborist who is skilled and equipped to efficiently remove trees. Never attempt to use a chainsaw without thorough knowledge of its safe use. Learn how to use a chainsaw properly by taking a course. Also, personal protection equipment must be worn. A chainsaw is a potentially lethal tool that should be

A tree that has a co-dominant stem with included bark, which made for a weak branch attachment split, probably in the wind, is now a hazard, and should be removed.

Have an arborist install cabling and bracing to help keep weak branch unions from splitting apart.

used with the utmost concern for safety. Don't attempt it, unless you are trained. Better yet, leave it to the experts!

Removing a tree stump requires the use of specialized equipment that can grind the stump down to well below the surface of the soil. Such machinery makes easy work of an otherwise extremely difficult and labor-intensive task. It is worth the money to hire an arborist with the equipment for this job.

4. Cabling/Bracing/Lightning Protection

Cabling and **bracing** are used to stabilize weak branch crotches and limbs to help reduce the risk of limbs or leaders from splitting apart, and may become necessary if young trees are neglected and allowed to mature with structural defects such as co-dominant leaders or branches with narrow crotch angles. Proper pruning when the tree is young will reduce the future need for cabling or bracing. As trees mature, cabling or bracing may become necessary to stabilize your tree and extend its life. Cabling involves the installation of flexible steel cables between tree limbs. The cables provide support and limit movement in leaders with poor crotches. They can also support long, heavy horizontal branches. Bracing is the use of steel rods in branches or the trunk to provide rigid support. Bracing reinforces weak or split crotches.

A bolt of lightning can blow a tree apart and inflict harm or damage to nearby objects. **Lightning protection** involves the installation of hardware in the tree to direct the electrical charge away from it. Lightning will strike an air terminal installed near the top of the tree, travel down a copper wire, and follow a 10-foot ground rod safely away from the tree. Consider installing lightning protection for historic trees, trees of economic value, any large trees within 10 feet of a structure, and trees in the open under which people often take refuge during a storm.

Arborists will recommend these services (cabling, bracing, lightning protection), and properly install the hardware. Installation may not be needed in some situations, so be sure that the advice you receive is consistent with what other tree specialists recommend.

5. Aeration and Fertilization
   Aeration and fertilization are often needed in urban environments.

   If your soil is lacking in required nutrients, your tree will show signs of nutrient deficiency. Nitrogen deficiencies show up in the foliage. Leaves may be smaller as growth is reduced and yellowing will occur. This can be corrected with fertilizer. A good application technique is **liquid injection**, a service provided by arborists. Fertilizer is mixed with water and injected under pressure into the soil. This process applies the fertilizer directly to the root zone, making it readily available for uptake by the tree. Consult your arborist.

6. Emergency Tree Care
   Storms can be harmful and destructive. Arborists can safely remove damaged or weak limbs, or an entire tree, and prevent further damage to your property.

7. Planting

Planting the wrong tree in the wrong location can lead to future problems caused by limited growing space, insects, diseases, or poor growth. Arborists can recommend appropriate trees for specific locations, and plant them correctly.

Bear in mind that some large tree care companies with arborists on staff have research laboratories backing them, so they can send soil samples for testing, and also diagnose disease and insect problems.

Guidelines for selecting an arborist

When selecting an arborist for tree work on your property, consider the following guidelines to make sure you hire the best person for the job:

- Have more than one arborist look at the job, and get a written bid specifying work to be done. Ask if cleanup is required, such as grinding of stump and surface roots, filling topsoil, etc.
- Ask for and check local references. Ask friends and neighbors for referrals.
- Beware of individuals who want to remove a living tree. This is sometimes necessary, but only as a last resort.
- Be wary of people who go door to door offering bargain tree work. Most reputable companies are too busy to do this.
- Low price is a poor gauge of a quality arborist. Often, better arborists are more expensive because they have more specialized equipment, offer more professional help, and carry sufficient insurance. The expense of proper care is an excellent investment. Pruning is an art, and skill and professionalism are more important than a low bid.
- Ask for certification of personal, property liability, and worker's compensation insurance, then phone the insurance company to make certain the policy is current. Many homeowners have had to pay out large sums of money for damages caused by uninsured individuals. You could be responsible for damages and injuries if you hire someone who is not insured.
- Some governmental agencies require contractors to apply for permits for tree work and/or apply for a license. Be sure to comply with any local, state, provincial, or national laws. Arborists in your area should be familiar with all such regulations, but double-check yourself!
- Good arborists use only accepted practices. For example, a conscientious arborist never uses climbing spikes unless the tree is to be removed. Avoid arborists who routinely top trees.
- Be wary of the claim of miracle cures.
- The condition of a firm's equipment often reflects its commitment to quality.

- Determine if the arborist is a member of the International Society of Arboriculture. Certification is attained after rigorous testing and several years' experience. Certification provides a measurable assessment of an individual's knowledge and competence. Certified arborists must also continue their education to maintain their certification. There are state and provincial chapters of the ISA throughout North America. Membership does not guarantee quality, but lack of membership casts doubt on the person's professionalism. Look for the ISA logo in the phone directory when you are searching for an arborist.
- Membership in professional organizations such as the ISA, the National Arborist Association (NAA) or the American Society of Consulting Arborists (ASCA) demonstrates an arborist's willingness to stay up to date on the latest techniques and developments in this field.

CONTACT INFORMATION

International Society of Arboriculture—www.isa-arbor.com
phone (217) 355-9411,
fax (217) 355-9516
From the website you can enter your zip code, postal code, or city to obtain a list of certified arborists in your area. Canadian chapters of the ISA are Ontario, Quebec, Pacific Northwest, Atlantic, and Prairie.

National Arborist Association—www.natlarb.com
phone (603) 314-5380,
fax (603) 314-5386
Membership comprises commercial tree care firms.

American Society of Consulting Arborists—www.asca-consultants.org
phone (301) 947-0483,
fax (301) 990-9771
Membership is made up of practising arborists who specialize in advising, diagnosing, recommending treatments, making appraisals, legal testimony, etc.

In addition, your local garden centers are also excellent sources of information, and they may be able to refer you to local certified arborists.

ISA Chapters
http://www.isa-arbor.com/ISAChapters/chapters.html

Please see the list below for websites of international ISA chapters. These websites will assist you in locating a certified arborist in your region.

Atlantic Chapter
(Canada—New Brunswick, Nova Scotia, Prince Edward Island, and Newfoundland)
For information e-mail isa@isa-arbor.com

Austria Chapter
For information e-mail isa@isa-arbor.com

Australia Chapter
http://home.vicnet.net.au/~isaa/

Brazil Chapter
For information e-mail isa@isa-arbor.com

Czech Republic Chapter
http://www.arboristika.cz/

Denmark Chapter
(Denmark, Finland, and Iceland)
http://www.dansk-traeplejeforening.dk/

Florida Chapter (US)
http://www.floridaisa.org/

French Chapter
http://www.siaz.org/sfa.html

Germany Chapter
For information e-mail isa@isa-arbor.com

Illinois Chapter (US)
http://www.illinoisarborist.org/

Indiana Chapter (US)
For information e-mail isa@isa-arbor.com

Italy Chapter
http://www.isaitalia.org/

Kentucky Chapter (US)
For information e-mail isa@isa-arbor.com

KPB Dutch Chapter
(The Netherlands)
For information e-mail isa@isa-arbor.com

Mexico Chapter
For information e-mail isa@isa-arbor.com

Michigan Chapter (US)
http://forestry.msu.edu/mfpa/index.htm

Mid-Atlantic Chapter
(US—Washington, DC, Maryland, Virginia, and West Virginia)
http://www.mac-isa.org/

Midwestern Chapter
(US—Iowa, Kansas, Missouri, Nebraska, North Dakota, Oklahoma, and South Dakota)
http://www.mwisa.unl.edu/

Minnesota Chapter (US)
http://www.isa-msa.org/pages/indexframes/intro.htm

New England Chapter
(US—Connecticut, Maine, Massachusetts, New Hampshire, Rhode Island, and Vermont)
http://www.newenglandisa.com/

New Jersey Chapter (US)
For information e-mail isa@isa-arbor.com

New York Chapter (US)
http://www.newyorkstatearborists.com/

New Zealand
http://www.nzarbor.org.nz/

Norway
http://www.norsk-trepleieforum.org/

Ohio Chapter (US)
http://www.ohiochapterisa.org/

Ontario Chapter (Canada)
http://www.isaontario.com/

Pacific Northwest Chapter
(US/Canada—Alaska, British Columbia, Idaho, Oregon, and Washington)
http://www.pnwisa.org/

Penn-Del Chapter
(US—Delaware and Pennsylvania)
http://www.penndelisa.org/

Prairie Chapter
(Canada—Alberta, Manitoba, and Saskatchewan)
For information e-mail isa@isa-arbor.com

Quebec Chapter (Canada)
http://www.siaq.org/

Rocky Mountain Chapter
(US—Colorado, Montana, New Mexico, and Wyoming)
http://www.isarmc.org/

Southern Chapter
(US—Alabama, Arkansas, Georgia, Louisiana, Mississippi, North Carolina, Puerto Rico, South Carolina, Tennessee, and Virgin Islands)
http://www.isasouthern.org/

Spain Chapter
http://www.aearboricultura.com/principa.htm

Texas Chapter (US)
http://www.trees-isa.org

United Kingdom/Ireland Chapter
(England, Ireland, Northern Ireland, Scotland, and Wales)
http://www.isa-uki.org/

Western Chapter
(US—Arizona, California, Hawaii, and Nevada)
http://www.wc-isa.net/front.asp

Wisconsin Chapter (US)
http://www.waa-isa.org/

The ISA website has a special site for consumers that provides Tree Care Information Brochures such as Tree Values, and Pruning Young Trees.
http://www2.champaign.isa-arbor.com/consumer/consumer.html

The National Arborist Association website also offers many tree tips.
http://www.vytc.com/treeTips.html

Many government bodies offer websites relating to tree care. These include federal sites, such as Natural Resources Canada, http://www.nrcan.gc.ca/cfs-scf/prodserv/tips_ehtml, and municipal sites, such as the cities of Chicago, http://www.ci.chi.il.us/Environment/CityTrees/, and Fort Worth, http://ci.fort-worth.tx.us/pacs/fwpacsd/forestry/fwtrees/fwtreemaint.htm.

The Tree Canada Foundation, a not-for-profit, charitable organization, is a leader in promoting the value of urban forests in Canada. Its website offers information about trees and tree care.
http://www.treecanada.ca/publications/guide.htm

PLACES AND ORGANIZATIONS

Here is a list of notable places to see locally native trees.

Adkins Arboretum
12610 Eveland Road, P.O. Box 100, Ridgely, MD 21660 US; 443-634-2847
http://www.hort.vt.edu/vthg/

Alaska Botanical Garden
P.O. Box 202202, Anchorage, AK 99520 US; 907-265-3165

Alfred B. Maclay State Gardens
3540 Thomasville Road, Tallahassee, FL 32308 US; 850-487-4115

Arboretum
University of Central Florida, c/o Dept. of Biology, Orlando, FL 32816-2368 US; 407-823-2978

Arboretum at Arizona State University
Facilities Management/Department Grounds, Tempe, AZ 85287-3305 US; 602-965-8137
http://www.fm.asu.edu/arboretum.htm

Arboretum at Flagstaff
P.O. Box 670, Flagstaff, AZ 86002 US; 520-774-1442
http://www.thearb.org/

Arboretum of Los Angeles County
301 N. Baldwin Avenue, Arcadia, CA 91007-2697 US;
626-821-3234
http://www.aabga.org/memberpages/losangeles/

Arboretum, University of Guelph
Guelph, ON N1G 2W1 Canada; 519-824-4120
http://www.uoguelph.ca/~arboretu/

Arizona-Sonora Desert Museum
2021 N. Kinney Road, Tucson, AZ 85743-8918 US; 520-883-1380
http://www.desertmuseum.org/

Arnold Arboretum
c/o Harvard University, 125 Arborway, Jamaica Plain, MA 02130-3500 US; 617-524-1718
http://www.arboretum.harvard.edu/

Atlanta Botanical Garden
P.O. Box 77246, Atlanta, GA 30357 US;
404-876-5859
http://www.atlantabotanicalgarden.org/

Beal Botanical Garden
Division of Campus Park & Planning, 412 Olds Hall, Office, East Lansing, MI 48824-1047 US; 517-355-9582
http://beal.cpp.msu.edu:80/beal/

Beardsley Zoological Gardens
1875 Noble Avenue, Bridgeport, CT 06610 US; 203-394-6569
http://www.BeardsleyZoo.org/

Bernheim Arboretum and Research Forest
Hwy. 245, Clermont, KY 40110 US;
502-955-8512
http://www.win.net/bernheim/

Berry Botanic Garden
11505 SW Summerville Avenue, Portland, OR 97219-8309 US; 503-636-4112
http://www.berrybot.org/

Betty Ford Alpine Gardens
183 Gore Creek Drive, Vail, CO 81657 US; 970-476-0103
http://www.vail.net/alpinegarden/

Biltmore Estate
One N. Pack Square, Asheville, NC 28801 US; 828-274-6202
http://www.biltmore.com/

Birmingham Botanical Gardens
2612 Lane Park Road, Birmingham, AL 35223 US; 205-879-1227
http://www.biltmore.com/

Botanica, The Wichita Gardens
701 N. Amidon, Wichita, KS 67203 US;
316-264-0448
http://www.botanica.org/

Boyce Thompson Southwestern Arboretum
37615 US 60, Superior, AZ 85273-5100 US;
520-689-2723
http://Ag.Arizona.Edu/BTA/

Brooklyn Botanic Garden
1000 Washington Avenue, Brooklyn,
NY 11225-1099 US; 718-622-4433
http://www.bbg.org/

Cape Fear Botanical Garden
P.O. Box 53485, Fayetteville, NC 28305 US;
910-486-0221

Cedar Valley Arboretum & Botanic Gardens
P.O. Box 1833, Waterloo, IA 50704 US;
319-296-9297
http://www.cedarnet.org/gardens/

Cheekwood Botanical Garden
1200 Forrest Park Drive, Nashville, TN 37205 US;
615-353-2148
http://www.aabga.org/memberpages/cheekwood/

Cheyenne Botanic Garden
710 S. Lions Park Drive, Cheyenne, WY 82001
US; 307-637-6458
http://www.botanic.org/

Chicago Botanic Garden
1000 Lake Cook Road, Glencoe, IL 60022 US;
847-835-5440
http://www.chicago-botanic.org/

Cincinnati Zoo and Botanical Garden
3400 Vine Street, Cincinnati, OH 45220 US;
513-559-7734
http://www.cincyzoo.org/

Cleveland Botanical Garden
11030 East Blvd., Cleveland, OH 44106 US;
216-721-1600

Crosby Arboretum, Mississippi State University
P.O. Box 1639, Picayune, MS 39466 US;
601-799-2311

Dawes Arboretum
7770 Jacksontown Road, SE, Newark, OH
43056-9380 US; 740-323-2355
http://www.dawesarb.org/

Denver Botanic Gardens
909 York Street, Denver, CO 80206 US;
303-331-4000
http://www.botanicgardens.org/

Desert Botanical Garden
1201 N. Galvin Pkwy., Phoenix, AZ 85008 US;
602-941-1225
http://www.dbg.org/

Dothan Area Botanical Gardens
P.O. Box 5971, Dothan, AL 36302 US;
334-793-3224
http://www.dabg.com/

Dyck Arboretum of the Plains
Hesston College, P.O. Box 3000, Hesston, KS
67062 US;
316-327-8127
http://erb.hesston.edu/arbor/

Florida Botanical Gardens
12175 125th Street North, Largo, FL 33774 US;
727-582-2100

Forest Lawn Cemetery & Arboretum
4000 Pilots Lane, Richmond, VA 23222 US;
804-321-7655

Fullerton Arboretum
c/o California State University, P.O. Box 6850,
Fullerton, CA 92834-6850 US; 714-278-3579
http://arboretum.fullerton.edu/home.htm

Garfield Park Botanical Conservatory
2505 Conservatory Drive, Indianapolis, IN 46203
US; 317-327-7184

Georgia Southern Botanical Garden
Georgia Southern University, P.O. Box 8039,
The Botanical Gardens, Statesboro, GA
30460-8039 US;
912-871-1114
http://www2.gasou.edu/garden/

Gifford Arboretum
University of Miami, Dept. of Biology, Cox Science
Center, Room 215, 1301 Memorial Drive, Coral
Gables, FL 33146 US;
305-284-5364
http://fig.cox.miami.edu/Arboretum/gifford.html

Graver Arboretum of Muhlenberg College
Biology Dept., 2400 Chew Street, Allentown, PA
18104-5586 US; 610-821-3258
http://www.muhlenberg.edu/

Green Bay Botanical Garden
2600 Larsen Road, P.O. Box 12644, Green Bay,
WI 54307-2644 US; 920-490-9457
http://www.uwm.edu/Dept/Biology/domes/

Haverford College Arboretum
Haverford College, 370 Lancaster Avenue,
Haverford, PA 19041 US; 610-896-1101
http://www.haverford.edu/

Hayes Regional Arboretum
801 Elks Road, Richmond, IN 47374 US;
765-962-3745
http://www.infocom.com/hayes/

Highland Botanical Park
180 Reservoir Avenue, Rochester, NY 14620 US;
716-244-9023

Highstead Arboretum
P.O. Box 1097, Redding, CT 06875 US;
203-938-8809

Hoyt Arboretum
Bureau of Parks, 4000 SW Fairview Blvd.,
Portland, OR 97221 US; 503-228-8733

Iowa Arboretum
1875 Peach Avenue, Madrid, IA 50156 US;
515-795-3216

J.C. Raulston Arboretum
P.O. Box 7609, Dept. of Horticultural Science,
North Carolina State University, Raleigh, NC
27695-7609 US; 919-515-1192

James Madison University Arboretum
MSU 6901, James Madison University,
Harrisonburg, VA 22807 US; 540-568-3194

Jardin Botanique de Montreal
4101, rue Sherbrooke Est, Montreal, PQ H1X 2B2
Canada;
514-872-1452

Leach Botanical Garden
6704 SE 122nd Avenue, Portland, OR 97236 US;
503-761-9503

Lockerly Arboretum
1534 Irwinton Road, Milledgeville, GA 31061 US;
912-452-2112

Marie Selby Botanical Gardens
811 S. Palm Avenue, Sarasota, FL 34236 US;
941-366-5731
http://www.selby.org/

Mary Grace Burns Arboretum
Georgian Court College, 900 Lakewood Avenue,
Lakewood, NJ 08701 US; 732-364-2200
http://www.Georgian.edu/bi_arbor/bi_arb.htm

Marywood University Arboretum
2300 Adams Avenue, Scranton, PA 18509 US;
717-348-6265

Matthaei Botanical Gardens
University of Michigan, 1800 N. Dixboro Road,
Ann Arbor, MI 48105 US; 734-998-7061
http://www.lsa.umich.edu/mbg/

**Memorial University of Newfoundland Botanical
Garden**
Memorial University of Newfoundland,
306 Mt. Scio Road, St. Johns, NF A1C 557 Canada;
709-737-8590
http://www.mun.ca/botgarden/

Memphis Botanic Garden
750 Cherry Road, Memphis, TN 38117-4699 US;
901-685-1566
http://www.aabga.org/memberpages/memphis/

Mendocino Coast Botanical Gardens
18220 N. Hwy. 1, Fort Bragg, CA 95437 US;
707-964-4352
http://www.fortbragg.com/gardens.htm

Mercer Arboretum & Botanic Gardens
22306 Aldine-Westfield Road, Humble, TX
77338-1071 US; 281-443-8731
http://www.cechouston.org/groups/memberguide.
html

Minnesota Landscape Arboretum
University of Minnesota, 3675 Arboretum Drive,
Box 39, Chanhassen, MN 55317 US; 612-443-2460
http://www.arboretum.umn.edu/fall_index.htm

Missouri Botanical Garden
P.O. Box 299, St. Louis, MO 63166-0299 US;
314-577-5111
http://www.mobot.org/

Morris Arboretum of the University of Pennsylvania
9414 Meadowbrook Avenue, Philadelphia, PA
19118 US; 215-247-5777
http://www.upenn.edu/morris/

Morton Arboretum
4100 Illinois Rte. 53, Lisle, IL 60532-1293 US;
630-968-0074
http://www.mortonarb.org/

Mount Auburn Cemetery
580 Mt. Auburn Street, Cambridge, MA 02138 US;
617-547-7105

Mount Pisgah Arboretum
33735 Seavey Loop Road, Eugene, OR 97405-9602
US; 541-747-3817
http://www.efn.org/~mtpisgah/

Mounts Botanical Garden
531 N. Military Trail, West Palm Beach, FL
33415-1395 US; 561-233-1749
http://www.mounts.org/

Myriad Botanical Gardens
100 Myriad Gardens, Oklahoma City, OK 73102
US; 405-297-3995
http://www.okccvb.org/myrgard/myrgard.html

Nebraska Statewide Arboretum
P.O. Box 830715, University of Nebraska, Lincoln,
NE 68583-0715 US; 402-472-2971
http://www.ianr.unl.edu/nsa/

New Orleans Botanical Garden
1 Palm Drive, New Orleans, LA 70124 US;
504-483-9386

New York Botanical Garden
200 Street & Kazimiroff Blvd., Bronx, NY
10458-5126 US; 718-817-8700
http://www.nybg.org/

Niagara Parks Botanical Gardens
P.O. Box 150, Niagara Falls, ON L2E 6T2 Canada;
905-356-8554
http://www.niagaraparks.com/

Nichols Arboretum
University of Michigan, Dana Bldg., 430 E.
University, Ann Arbor, MI 48109-1115 US;
734-763-4033
http://www.umich.edu/~snrewww/arb/

Norfolk Botanical Garden
6700 Azalea Garden Road, Norfolk, VA
23518-5337 US; 757-441-5830

North Carolina Arboretum
100 Frederick Law Olmsted Way, Asheville, NC
28806-9315 US; 828-665-2492

North Carolina Botanical Garden
University of North Carolina at Chapel Hill, CB
3375, Totten Center, Chapel Hill, NC 27599-3375
US; 919-962-0522
http://www.unc.edu/depts/ncbg/

Ohio State University Chadwick Arboretum
2001 Fyffe Court, Columbus, OH 43210 US;
614-292-4678

Oklahoma Botanical Garden & Arboretum
OK State University, Hort. & L.A.
360 Agriculture Hall, Stillwater, OK 74078-6027
US; 405-744-5414

Omaha Botanical Gardens
P.O. Box 24089, Omaha, NE 68124 US;
402-346-4002

Orland E. White Arboretum
State Arboretum of Virginia, Rt. 2, Box 210, Boyce,
VA 22620 US; 540-837-1758
http://www.virginia.edu/~blandy/

Overland Park Arboretum & Botanical Garden
8500 Santa Fe, Overland Park, KS 66212 US;
913-685-3604

Red Butte Garden and Arboretum
University of Utah, 18A deTrobriand Street, Salt
Lake City, UT 84113-5044 US; 801-581-4747
http://www.utah.edu/redbutte/

Reeves-Reed Arboretum
165 Hobart Avenue, Summit, NJ 07901 US;
908-273-8787
http://www.reeves-reedarboretum.org/

Reflection Riding Arboretum and Botanical Garden
400 Garden Road, Chattanooga, TN 37419 US;
423-821-9582
http://www.chattanooga.net/rriding/

Reiman Gardens
Iowa State University, 1407 Elwood Drive, Ames,
IA 50011 US; 515-294-3718

Royal Botanical Gardens
P.O. Box 399, Hamilton, ON L8N 3H8 Canada;
905-527-1158
http://www.rbg.ca/

Salisbury State University Arboretum
1101 Camden Avenue, Salisbury, MD 21801 US;
443-543-6323
http://www.ssu.edu/

San Antonio Botanical Gardens
555 Funston Place, San Antonio, TX 78209 US;
210-207-3255
http://www.sabot.org/

Santa Barbara Botanic Garden
1212 Mission Canyon Road, Santa Barbara, CA
93105 US; 805-682-4726
http://www.sbbg.org/

Santa Fe Botanical Garden
P.O. Box 23343, Santa Fe, NM 87502-3343 US;
505-428-1684

Sarah P. Duke Gardens
Duke University, Box 90341, Durham, NC
27708-0341 US; 919-684-3698
http://www.hr.duke.edu/dukegardens/
dukegardens.html

Scott Arboretum of Swarthmore College
500 College Avenue, Swarthmore, PA 19081-1397
US; 610-328-8025

Secrest Arboretum
OARDC/OSU, 1680 Madison Avenue, Wooster,
OH 44691 US; 330-263-3761

Sherwood Fox Arboretum
Staging Bldg., University of Western Ontario,
London, ON N6A 5B7 Canada; 519-679-2111

Slayton Arboretum of Hillsdale College
Dept. of Biology, Hillsdale, MI 49242 US;
517-437-7341
http://www.aabga.org/memberpages/slayton/

South Carolina Botanical Garden
130 Lehotsky Hall, Clemson University, Public
Service & Agriculture, Clemson, SC 29634-0375
US; 864-656-3405
http://virtual.clemson.edu/groups/scbg/

State Botanical Garden of Georgia
University of Georgia, 2450 S. Milledge Avenue,
Athens, GA 30605 US; 706-542-1244
http://www.uga.edu/~botgarden/

State Fair Park Arboretum
Nebraska State Board of Agriculture, P.O. Box
81223, Lincoln, NE 68501 US; 402-474-5371

Stranahan Arboretum
Dept. of Biology, The University of Toledo, Toledo,
OH 43606-3390 US; 419-882-6806

Strybing Arboretum & Botanical Gardens
9th Avenue & Lincoln Way, San Francisco, CA
94122 US; 415-661-1316
http://www.strybing.org/

Taylor Memorial Arboretum
10 Ridley Drive, Wallingford, PA 19086 US;
610-876-2649
http://www.aabga.org/memberpages/taylor/

Toledo Botanical Garden
5403 Elmer Drive, Toledo, OH 43615 US;
419-936-2986

Toronto Zoo
361A Old Finch Avenue, Scarborough, ON
M1B 5K7 Canada; 416-392-5973
http://www.torontozoo.com/

Tucson Botanical Gardens
2150 N. Alvernon Way, Tucson, AZ 85712 US;
520-326-9686
http://www.azstarnet.com/~tbg/

Tyler Arboretum
515 Painter Road, Media, PA 19063 US;
610-566-9134

UC Davis Arboretum
University of California, One Shields Avenue, Davis, CA 95616 US; 530-752-2498

UCI Arboretum
North Campus, UC Irvine, Irvine, CA 92697-1450 US; 949-824-5833

United States National Arboretum
3501 New York Avenue, NE, Washington, DC 20002-1958 US; 202-245-2726

University of Alberta Devonian Botanic Garden
Edmonton, AB T6G 2E1 Canada; 403-987-3054

University of British Columbia Botanical Garden
6804 SW Marine Drive, Vancouver, BC V6T 1Z4 Canada; 604-822-3928
http://www.hedgerows.com/

University of California Botanical Garden
200 Centennial Drive, #5045, Berkeley, CA 94720-5045 US; 510-642-0849

University of California-Riverside Botanic Garden,
Riverside, CA 92521-0124 US; 909-787-4650

University of California Santa Cruz Arboretum
Arboretum UCSC, 1156 High Street, Santa Cruz, CA 95064 US; 381-427-2998

University of Delaware Botanic Gardens
Dept. of Plant & Soil Science, University of Delaware, Newark, DE 19717 US; 302-831-1388

University of Idaho Arboretum & Botanical Garden
109-110 Alumni Center, Moscow, ID 83844-3226 US; 208-885-6250

University of Illinois Arboretum
205 Swanlund Administration Bldg., 601 E. John Street, Champaign, IL 61820 US; 217-333-8846

University of Kentucky Arboretum
University of Kentucky, Room 8, Gillis Bldg., Lexington, KY 40506-0033 US; 606-257-6955
http://www.uky.edu/OtherOrgs/Arboretum/

University of NE-Lincoln Botanical Garden & Arboretum
1340 N. 17th Street, Lincoln, NE 68588-0609 US; 402-472-2679
http://www.unl.edu/unlbga/

University of Wisconsin Arboretum
1207 Seminole Hwy., Madison, WI 53711 US; 608-262-2746

US Botanic Garden
Administrative Office, 245 First Street, SW, Washington, DC 20024 US; 202-225-8333

VanDusen Botanical Garden
5251 Oak Street, Vancouver, BC V6M 4H1 Canada; 604-257-8666

Washington Park Arboretum
University of Washington, P.O. Box 358010, Seattle, WA 98195-8010 US; 206-543-8800

GLOSSARY

abiotic plant problem—caused by non-living agents such as weather conditions, soil conditions, and man-made physical and chemical disturbances to the air and environment

acid soil—has a pH less than 7.0

alkaline soil—has a pH of more than 7.0

annual rings—the rings of wood laid down each year after the burst of spring growth; visible in the cross-section of a tree's trunk

apical dominance—condition in which the bud on the end of a twig or shoot inhibits the growth and development of lateral buds on the same stem

arboriculture—the study of trees and other plants

arborist—a qualified specialist in the care of trees

backfill—soil put back into the planting hole

bareroot—tree with an exposed root system without soil

biotic plant problem—caused by living agents, such as insects, and diseases such as fungi, bacteria, and viruses

boring insect—insect larvae such as the European bark beetle that tunnel under a tree's bark and into the wood

bracing—installation of metal rods through weak portions of a tree for added support

branch collar—area where branch joins another branch or trunk, sometimes identified by swelling where the branch meets the trunk

branch union/crotch—a point where branch originates from the trunk or another branch

bud—small protuberance on the stem of a plant that may develop into a flower or shoot

cabling—installation of hardware in a tree to help support weak branches or crotches caliche—soil heavy in alkaline

caliper—measurement of the diameter of a tree's trunk

callus—tissue formed by the cambium layer around and over a wound

candles—light-colored, softer new growth on the branch ends of evergreens

canker—localized diseased area, often shrunken and discolored, on trunk and branches

central/dominant leader—the main stem of a tree

chemical pesticide—control measure used to combat persistent insect and disease problems, somtimes toxic

chewing insect—also called defoliators and leaf miners, these are insects such as the gypsy moth that eat plant tissue

chlorophyll—green pigment concentrated in outer leaf tissues

CODIT—compartmentalization of decay in trees

compartmentalization—natural process of defense in trees by which they wall off decay in the wood

competing leader—stem competing with central stem of a tree

complete fertilizer—fertilizer that contains nitrogen, phosphorus, and potassium

conifer—a cone-bearing tree such as pine, spruce, or cedar

controlled-release fertilizer—made up of soluble granules encased with a permeable coating released through watering

cork/bark cambium—layers of cells that give rise to the cork and bark

corrective pruning—activity such as pruning interfering limbs, poorly spaced limbs, and weak crotches

cracks—defects in a tree that may pose a risk of tree or branch failure

crown—the aboveground portions of a tree (also referred to as canopy)

crown restoration—method of restoring the natural growth habit of a tree that has been topped or damaged in a storm

cultivar—a tree cultivated to produce specific desirable features such as foliage color and height

cultural control—a method of controlling plant problems by providing a growing environment that is favorable to the host plant and/or unfavorable to the pest

deciduous—trees and shrubs that shed all of their foliage during fall to prepare for dormancy during winter

dieback—any plant part, usually ends of branches, that is dying

dormant—state of reduced physiological activity in the organs of a plant

drip line—perimeter of the area under a tree's crown

dwarf tree—term that refers to trees smaller than the usual size for a particular species

evergreen—having green foliage throughout the year

fertilizer—substance added to a plant or surrounding soil to supplement the supply of essential elements

flagging—dead, dropping branch, with discolored foliage

foliage—the leaves of a plant

flush cut—removal of a branch right to the trunk, leaving no stub, and removing the natural protection zone of a tree

girdling—inhibitor of flow of the water and nutrients in a tree by "choking" root tissues

girdling roots—roots located above or below ground level whose circular growth around the base of the trunk or over individual roots applies pressure to the bark area, thereby choking or restricting the flow of water and nutrients

glazing—occurs when the sides or bottom of the planting hole become smooth, forming a barrier through which water has difficulty passing

graft—a shoot or bud of one plant inserted into the stem or trunk of another

guying—securing a tree with ropes or cable fastened to stakes in the ground

hardiness zone rating—the accepted standard of determining the hardiness of a particular plant

hardiness zone—preferred growing conditions of a particular plant

hawthorn rust—a disease that affects foliage, characterized by rusty spots on leaves

heartwood—non-functional xylem tissues that help support the trunk

heat island effect—phenomenon caused when the sun beats down on concrete and asphalt in the city, increasing temperatures by up to 9 degrees

honeydew—sticky, sugary secretion deposited on leaves and stems by insects such as aphids and whiteflies

horticultural oil—non-toxic alternative pesticide

included bark—bark that is pushed inside a developing crotch, causing a weakened structure

insecticidal soap—non-toxic insecticide soap spray

integrated pest management (IPM)—a systematic approach to insect and disease management

interfering limbs—limbs that cross each other or rub against one another

lac balsam—a natural substance used as a cosmetic repair to trunk damage resulting from broken or torn limbs

lateral branch—secondary branch

leach—tendency for elements to wash down through the soil

leaf scorch—browning or shriveling of foliage, usually caused by drought where sunshine and drying winds stimulate water loss from leaves

lenticels—elongated pores in a tree's bark that permit exchange of gases

lightning protection—installation of hardware in a tree to direct electrical charge away from it

lion tailing—stripping of branches of their lateral limbs, leaving growth only on the ends of the branches

microclimate—areas within a garden where climate is modified. Warm microclimates, usually near tall trees, hedges, fences, and walls, are sometimes suitable for tender or out-of-zone plants.

mulch—organic matter such as wood chips spread on the ground around trees to prevent the evaporation of water and to provide insulation against the cold

mycorrhizae—a fungus that form a symbiotic relationship with tree roots

native species—indigenous to a region

oasis effect—phenomenon caused when wind moves through a shade canopy or stand of trees, cooling the air under a shade tree by as much as 10 degrees

out-of-zone—a tree planted in an area outside its optimum hardiness zone

photosynthesis—process by which light energy is used to combine carbon dioxide and water to produce sugar and oxygen

pith—central core of early growth in twigs

phloem—thin layer of cells inside bark that carry carbohydrates produced by leaves to all the living tissue

pH—a measure of acidity or alkalinity in soil

powdery mildew—white, powdery patches caused by a certain fungus that appear on leaves if they become overcrowded and the soil is dry

primary nutrients—nitrogen (N), phosphorous (P), and potassium (K)

prune—to purposefully cut and remove parts of a tree for a specific reason

root ball—containment of roots and soil of a tree

root bound—condition of roots of trees that have been grown in pots with inadequate room for root growth and movement

root burn—condition of roots of trees that have been grown in pots with inadequate room for root growth and movement

root collar—usually at or near the ground line, and identifiable as a marked swelling of the tree trunk

sapwood—outer wood that transports water, oxygen, and minerals

scaffold branches—the permanent or structural branches of a tree

secateurs—bypass-style pruning shears used on small trees and shrubs to make cuts up to 1/2 inch in diameter

shade tree—large tree, usually deciduous, that provides ample shade as a result of its size

shearing—removal of a portion of current season's growth on a shrub

skeletonizing—characterized by removal of leaf tissues between the leaf veins

soil amendment—material added to soil to improve its physical or chemical properties

soil analysis—laboratory analysis of soil to determine pH and mineral composition

soil compaction—soil compressed by heavy equipment or other means resulting in reduction of total pore space

stomata—tiny pores in leaves that allow gases to be exchanged

stub—what remains of a branch after it's been cut

sucker—shoot arising from the base of a tree

sucking insect—insects such as aphids and mites that penetrate and feeds on plant juices by sucking out sap

sunscald—occurs when living bark tissue dehydrates and dies from exposure to bright, intense winter sun, or when water in thawed bark cells refreezes and expands at night, destroying the cells

thinning—selective removal of unwanted branches and limbs to provide light and air penetration through the tree or to lighten the weight of the remaining limbs

topping—cutting back a tree to buds, stubs, or laterals not large enough to assume dominance

transplant—to move a plant to a new location

tree spade—mechanical device used to dig and move trees

upright branches—branches that grow straight up, rather than outward

U-shaped crotch/fork—stronger branch union than V-shaped crotch

V-shaped crotch/fork—poor branch attachment or co-dominant stem, a weak crotch that is likely to have included bark (common in silver maple)

vascular tissue—tissues that conduct water or nutrients

vertical mulching—method used to relieve compacted soil, which involves drilling holes every few feet to a depth of approximately 12 inches and backfilling with organic matter such as peat moss

verticillium wilt—a fungus that inhabits surrounding soil and invades and plugs water-conducting tissue, shutting off water supply to top growth

vista pruning—removal of branches to allow for a specific view (e.g., view of lake from cottage deck)

water shoot (or sprout)—a secondary, upright shoot arising from the trunk or branches of a plant

xylem—transports water, oxygen, and nutrients up from the roots to the branches and leaves

REFERENCES

In writing this book, we relied heavily on information provided by the International Society of Arboriculture, especially ISA Tree Care Information brochures, the *Aborists' Certification Study Guide*, and *Barlett Tree Experts' Course in Arboriculture*.

Adam, Judith. *Landscape Planning: Practical Techniques for the Home Gardener*. Toronto, ON: Firefly Books, 2002.

Appleton, Bonnie Lee. *Rodale's Successful Organic Gardening: Trees, Shrubs & Vines*. Plant Guide by Alfred F. Scheider. Emmaus, PN: Rodale Press, 1993.

Bartlett Tree Experts Course in Arboriculture. Barlett Tree Research Laboratories in cooperation with the International Society of Arboriculture, Bartlett Tree Research Laboratories, Charlotte, NC, 1999.

Benvie, Sam. *The Encyclopedia of Trees: Canada and the United States*. Toronto, ON: Key Porter Books, 1999.

Brochures prepared by the Council of Tree and Landscape, developed by the International Society of Arboriculture, 1994: Benefits of Trees, Buying High-Quality Trees, Insect and Disease Problems, Mature Tree Care, Plant Health Care Recognizing Tree Hazards, Treatment of Trees Damaged by Construction, Tree Selection, Tree Values, Why Hire an Arborist, Why Topping Hurts Trees.

Bruce, Ian. "Standard Pruning" and "Hazard Tree Management" course notes, Humber College, Toronto, ON, 1996.

Buchanan, Rita. "Caring for Your Trees." *Country Living Gardener*, October 2000, Vol. 8, No. 5, pp. 93–100.

Carbon, Chris R. "Mulch, Park 2: Go Wide, Not Deep." *International Society of Arboriculture Arborist News*, Volume II Number 1 (2002): 35–39.

"City Trees: How to plant a tree." Chicago Dept. of Environment, 1998, http://w15.cityofchicago.org./environment/CityTrees/Planting.html

"City Trees: Construction areas." Chicago Dept. of Environment, 1998, http://w15.cityofchicago.org./environment/CityTrees/Construction.html

Cole, Trevor. *Gardening with Trees & Shrubs in Ontario, Quebec, & the Northeastern U.S.* Vancouver/Toronto: Whitecap Books, 1996.

Dirr, Michael A. *Manual of Woody Landscape Plants: Their Identification, Ornamental Characteristics, Culture, and Propagation and Uses.* Champaign, IL: Stipes Publishing L.L.C., 1998.

Farrar, John Laird. *Trees in Canada.* Fitzhenry & Whiteside Limited and the Canadian Forest Service Natural Resources Canada in cooperation with the Canada Communication Group—Publishing Supply and Services Canada, Markham, ON, 1995.

Fitzpatrick, Mike. "Protect Trees and Increase Property Value with Tree Preservation." *International Society of Arboriculture Arborist News,* Volume II Number 3 (2002): 58–60.

Heimann, M.F., O.S.F Boone, and D.M. Boone, "Disorder: Black Knot Plum and Cherry," St. Louis Park, MN: Rainbow Treecare, date unknown.

Hessayon, Dr. D.G. *The Tree & Shrub Expert.* London: Transworld Publishers, 2001.

Hole, Jim. "Prudent Pruning," *National Post,* April 7, 2001, W22.

Hole, Lois. *Lois Hole's Favorite Trees & Shrubs.* Edmonton, AB: Lone Pine Publishing, 1997.

Ip, D.W. Forestry Leaflet 19: Dutch Elm Disease, Forestry Canada, Ministry of Supply and Services Canada, 1992.

Johnson, Gary R. "Protecting Trees from Construction Damage: A Homeowner's Guide." Regents of the University of Minnesota, 1999, http://www.extension.umn.edu/distribution/ housingandclothing/DK613.html

Johnson, Jan and John C. Fech. *Ortho's All About Trees.* Des Moines, IW: Meredith Books, 1999.

Kershaw, Linda. *Trees of Ontario.* Edmonton, AB: Lone Pine Publishing, 2001.

Kessell, Christopher. "Juniper & Diplodia Tip Dieback." Ontario Ministry of Agriculture, Food & Rural Affairs, *OSTC News,* Volume II, Number 3, Summer, 1994.

Lily, Sharon J. *Arborists' Certification Study Guide.* Sharon J. Lilly, Champaign, IL: International Society of Arboriculture, 2001.

Nursery & Landscape Plant Production, Publication 383, Ontario Ministry of Agriculture, Food and Rural Affairs, 2000.

Obrizok, Robert A. *A Garden of Conifers: Introduction and Selection Guide.* Deer Park, WI: Capability's Books, 1994.

Ontario Extension Notes "Maintaining Healthy Urban Trees," Land Owner Resource Centre, http.www.lrconline.com/Extension_Notes_English/pdf/urbntrs.pdf

Osborne, Robert. *Hardy Trees and Shrubs: A Guide to Disease-Resistant Varieties for the North.* Photography by Beth Powning. Toronto, ON: Key Porter Books, 1996.

Pirone, P.P., J.R. Hartman, M.A. Sall, and T.P. Pirone. *Tree Maintenance.* New York, NY: Oxford University Press, 2001.

Smiley, Thomas, Sharon Lilly, and Patrick Kelsey. "Fertlizing Trees and Shrubs Part 1: Determining if, When, and What to Use." *International Society of Arboriculture Arborist News,* Volume II Number 2 (2002): 17–22.

"Some Tips on How to Care for Damaged Trees." Canadian Forest Service, Natural Resources Canada, http://www.nrcan.gc.ca/cfs-scf/science/prodserv/tips_e.html

Sternberg, Guy, and Jim Wilson. *Landscaping with Native Trees: The Northeast, Midwest, Midsouth & Southeast Edition.* Shelbourne, VT: Chapters Publishing Ltd., 1995.

Stienstra, Ward. "Apple Scab," Plant Pathology, AG-FS-1173, Minnesota Extension Service, University of Minnesota, date unknown.

———, and Dale R. Gergdahl. "Spruce and Their Diseases." University of Minnesota, date unknown.

Sunset Books and Sunset Magazine eds. *Sunset Trees & Shrubs: A-Z Encyclopedia, Planting & Care, Plant Selection Guide.* Menlo Park, CA: Sunset Publishing Corporation, 1994.

Tanenbaum, Frances, ed. *Taylor's 50 Best Trees: Easy Plants for More Beautiful Gardens.* Boston, MA/New York, NY: Houghton Mifflin Company, 1999.

Tucker, Patrick J. "Arboriculture—Chapter IV" of Horticulture I, course #191 (1991), Independent Study division, University of Guelph, Guelph, ON.

White, Hazel. *Small-Tree Gardens: Simple Projects, Contemporary Designs.* San Francisco, CA: Chronicle Books, 2000.

Whitman, Ann H., ed. *National Audubon Society Pocket Guide: Familiar Trees of North America East.* New York, NY: Alfred A. Knopf, 1986.

ACKNOWLEDGMENTS

We are grateful to the hard-working staff of Key Porter Books for supporting this book.

We thank Patricia Thomson for reviewing the manuscript.

We also wish to acknowledge our teachers, especially those at the University of Guelph, Humber College, and Simon Fraser University.

INDEX

Page citations in **boldface** below refer to **illustrations**.
Page citations in *italic* below refer to *glossary* definitions and explanations.